Success with
Houseplants

GISELA KEIL

Series Editor

LESLEY YOUNG

MEREHURST

Introduction

It is not surprising that houseplants are now more popular than ever before. They are able to bring a little magic to your home or office, giving even the most sober and boring room a touch of greenery or a hint of colour and scent, or creating an exotic mood. Many people like to keep houseplants but very few really know what they need in the way of vital care. Often bought on the spur of the moment, many plants soon lose first their beauty, then their lives. This is when you need help – and here it is. This useful guide covers the care of houseplants right down to the basics. It is concise, informative and essentially practical. In this book the author offers advice that will ensure success for beginners or more experienced houseplant owners – whether at home or in the office. Just open the book at the relevant place and follow the instructions.
In this guide you will discover what it is that houseplants really need in order to thrive and produce healthy foliage and beautiful flowers – the right position in a room, the right amount of watering and fertilizing and repotting at the right time. In addition, there are tables giving tips on care for 100 of the most popular flowering and green houseplants. Excellent colour photographs will help you to identify plants and to choose your favourites.

Contents

A weekend supply of water. Cotton wicks conduct moisture to the pots.

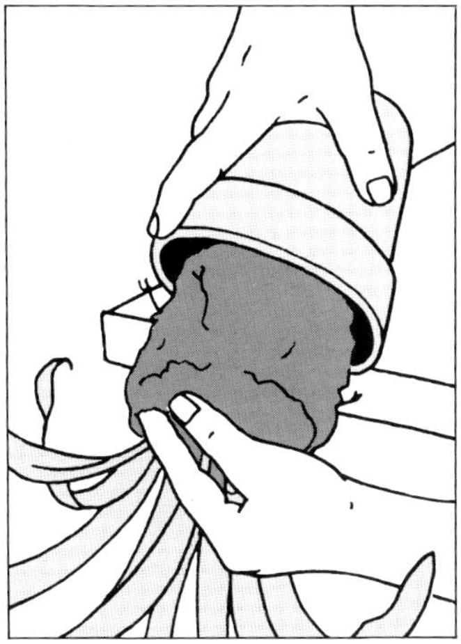

Repotting tip: *Tap the upside-down pot against the edge of the table to loosen the roots.*

The author
Gisela Keil is a student of education and psychology and of German, English and comparative literature. An author of gardening books for many years, she has been an enthusiastic houseplant keeper for twenty years and also spends a great deal of time in her wild garden and on promoting "green" gardening methods.

The photographers
Ulrike Schneiders trained as a photographer at the Bavarian Institute for Photography and also worked with her father, Toni Schneiders. She has worked professionally for calendar and art publishers since 1978, with a special emphasis on flowers, landscapes and still life. The majority of the photographs in this guide were taken by her. The other photographs were taken by other well-known plant photographers (see p. 63).

The illustrator
After studying at the Academy of Art in Budapest, György Jankovics attended the Academy of Art in Hamburg. He then trained as a technical artist and subsequently worked for several well-known publishing companies. For a number of years he has been an acclaimed illustrator of books on animals and plants.

Important
Please read the Author's note on the inside back cover to ensure that your enjoyment of houseplants is not spoiled in any way.

The requirements of houseplants vary as much as their appearance. Light, temperature and humidity can all be measured indoors and, if necessary, adapted to suit the requirements of individual plants.

Position

The secret of success with houseplants lies in the choice of the right position. When choosing a position for your plants, look for a spot that will provide, as far as possible, the same conditions in respect of light, air and temperature that they would enjoy in their country of origin. Once you have done this, all other care is mere child's play.

Position

What are houseplants?

Nature did not invent houseplants as there are no closed rooms in the wild. It was people who first began, thousands of years ago, to bring plants of all kinds into their living areas. But what is the attraction of such plants?

- Houseplants nearly all originate from tropical or subtropical regions.
- They are not usually hardy or frost-resistant and would not survive outside in temperate climates.
- They are dependent on being grown in containers indoors.
- They enchant us with the beauty of their leaves and flowers or with their interesting shapes.
- Nearly all of them are in leaf all year round.
- Many houseplants are no longer pure species, as in nature, but have been developed from hybrids etc. Generally, the following goals have been sought: longer flowering times; larger, more intensely coloured, multi-coloured or double flowers; better chances of survival indoors and a decreased susceptibility to pests and diseases.

Masters of adaptation

Like all other plants, the plants that we keep indoors have resulted from millions of years of specialization in growing in certain climates and positions and have developed a multitude of techniques to enable them to survive. Over time, they have adapted so well to the prevailing conditions in their places of origin that these special characteristics have become part of their genetic programming. Among the more relevant conditions for maintaining healthy growth, the most important are the timing and amount of warmth, water, humidity and nutrients (see p. 16).

Appearance and shape of growth: The overall shape of plants, be it the shape and size of their leaves, the characteristics of their flowers and roots or their upright, climbing, prostrate or pendulous growth, is one way in which plants have adapted to their position in the wild, with the sole aim of surviving and reproducing.

Growth cycle: This also evolved through the adaptation of plants to the conditions of their original climate. Few species will form buds and flowers if you do not observe their preferred phases of growth and rest.

- Growth periods are usually restricted to times of maximum warmth, allied to plenty of light and moisture. This is when plants form shoots and produce flowers.
- Rest phases usually occur during times of drought or in the cooler, darker time of year when growth ceases. In the case of bulbous or tuberous plants, this is the time when the leaves will turn yellow and the plants will die back, storing nutrients in their underground organs.

My tip: In temperate climates, most houseplants have a rest phase during the winter, as do most native plants.
Where this is not the case, the individual needs of plants must be taken into consideration – for example, a cooler, shadier position, little water, no fertilizer – all at the right time. Plants from tropical rain forests have no natural rest phase. They are, however, forced to undergo a rest phase in temperate climates where there is a decrease of light in the winter. Try to give them as bright a position as possible during this time and water them sparingly.

The country of origin is a decisive factor

Tropical plants come from very varying climatic zones.

- Rain forest plants (such as maidenhair fern, *Adiantum tenerum*) are used to heavy rainfall without dry periods, high humidity and cool nights. When kept indoors, they will not such as full sunlight or dry air and do not require a rest phase.
- Plants from savannahs and steppes (such as *Pentas lanceolata*) have adapted to alternating rainy and dry seasons. They will require a rest phase corresponding to a natural dry season.
- Plants from tropical mountain forests (such as *Camellia*) like very bright light with lots of rain, mist and cool temperatures. When kept indoors, tropical mountain plants will require a combination of plenty of light, high humidity and cool temperatures.
- Plants from desert regions, such as cacti, can cope with any amount of sunlight, high temperatures and drought. Indoors, they will require plenty of light all year round. During the winter, they must have cool temperatures and dry conditions, otherwise they will not produce any flowers.

Subtropical plants have adapted to hot summers and mild winters. Representatives from regions that receive summer rain need a rest period during the winter and to be placed in a cool, dry position. Plants from regions that receive rain in winter need light, warmth and plenty of water during the winter.

How plants live

The roots supply water and nutrients and anchor the plant firmly in the soil. Many roots are also able to store the starch produced by the plant or to retain it in enlarged organs, like rhizomes, tubers or bulbs, until needed.
Depending on the plant, the shoots can be leafy-green or brown and woody. They contain vascular tissue which conducts water and nutrients from the roots to the leaves of the plants.
The leaves are equivalent to the lung and the digestive organs of humans. Most of the respiration, the photosynthesis and the processing of nutrients take place in the leaves (see illustration, right).
The flowers are only a transitional phase for the plant, indicating its readiness for reproduction.

Care of plants

Houseplants can be divided into two groups: flowering plants and plants with attractive foliage. The following pages will tell you how plants in these two groups should be cared for.

The metabolic processes of plants by day

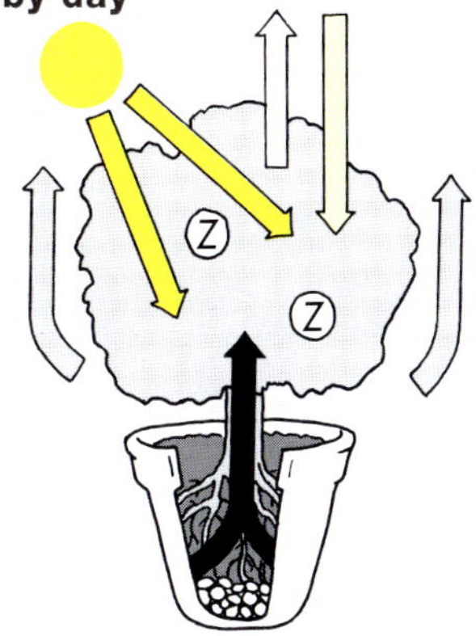

1. Photosynthesis: This process is only possible because of the green pigment called chlorophyll, which is contained in the leaves. Sunlight causes the plant to absorb carbon dioxide (CO_2) from the air and, with the help of water, transforms this gas into carbohydrates (sugar). During the process, the plant releases oxygen (O) into the air.
2. Assimilation: Together with nutrients, the carbohydrates are transformed into the basic building elements of plants and then conducted to the growth zones of the plant or held in storage organs.
3. Respiration (see right-hand column): Respiration and photosynthesis occur simultaneously during the day.
4. Transpiration (see right-hand column): Under the influence of sunlight and the sun's warmth, plants release more moisture (H_2O) through evaporation during the daytime than at night.

The metabolic processes of plants by night

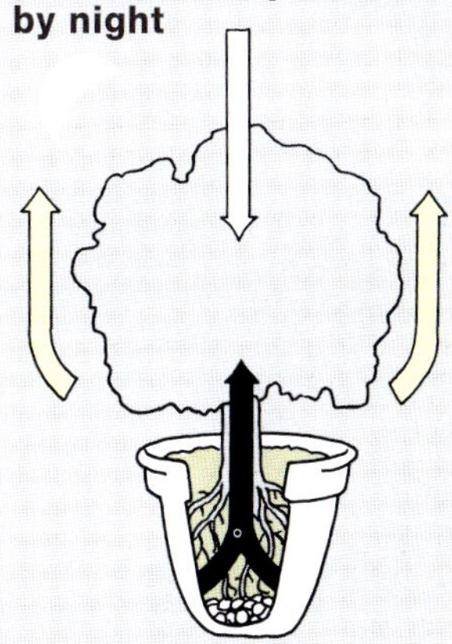

1. Respiration: Through their pores, the leaves absorb oxygen (O) from the air and also release carbon dioxide (CO_2). Carbohydrates stored during the day are partly released again during this process.
2. Transpiration: Like many other living things, plants "perspire" when the temperature rises by releasing moisture through their leaves. This creates a certain moisture deficiency and a strong suction effect from below, which enables the roots to suck up the necessary amount of moisture. If more moisture is evaporated through the leaves than the roots are able to replenish, the plant will become limp.
A further advantage is that transpiration also helps the plant to cool its leaves.
When temperatures drop at night, the plant transpires less. When the weather is dull and cool, watering should be cut down.

Flowering plants and their care

A beginners' orchid: Phalaenopsis.

Flowering time
If you wish, you can surround yourself with flowering plants all year round, although this is only possible with species that flower at different times, one after the other. The length of plants' flowering times can vary just as much as the time each flower lasts. Some plants have flowers that last for just one day; others last for weeks.

African violets.

Easter cactus is also suitable for hanging containers.

The flower
Flowering plants are the most popular houseplants, even though the flowers appear for a relatively short time. When the flowerbuds start forming, the plant is reaching maturity. All its energies now go into fertilization so that it can produce fruits or seeds. Plants invest an inordinate amount of energy in this process.
My tip: If you want to keep flowers blooming for as long as possible, you should cut off any dead heads as soon as you can to prevent the plant using up energy unnecessarily.

A bulbous plant: Hippeastrum.

Orchids
Orchids will generally only produce flowers if great attention is given to their natural growth cycles.
Late winter/spring: The amount of light and water should be increased at the beginning of the growth phase.
Early spring/summer: Water and fertilize regularly. This is the growth phase.
Late summer/autumn: Lower the temperature by at least 4–6° C (39–43° F) at night, water less, but allow plenty of light. This is the time of bud formation.
Autumn/winter: Rest and flowering times. Give more light but not very much water.

Cacti
There are countless species of cacti, many of which have quite different requirements.
Desert cacti (see photograph, p. 41), like a bright position all year round.

- full sunlight in the summer, fresh air and plenty of water as well as sparse amounts of fertilizer containing very little nitrogen;
- in the autumn, bright, but no sunlight; at 5–12° C (41–54° F), do not water anymore;
- in the spring, cautiously begin watering again.

Exceptions: The warmth-loving disco and melon cacti which can overwinter in heated rooms.

The bromeliad Aechmea.

In spite of its delicate flowers, the blue passion flower (Passiflora caerulea) is quite robust and will produce shoots up to 1 m (40 in) long in one year. It is overwintered like a large container plant: in a bright, cool position

Care at a glance

	Name	Flowering time	Light	Watering	Humidity	Fertilizing	Further tips on care
●	*Adenium* desert rose ☠	IV–VIII	☼			every fortnight: III–VIII cactus fertilizer	compost, hydroculture; O: around 15° C/59° F, cool, dry.
	Aechmea (bromeliad)	V–X flowers once	○		✓	every fortnight: III–VIII	compost, hydroculture, some epiphytic; O:18–25° C/64–77° F.
	Aeschynanthus	V–VIII	○		✓	fortnightly: III–VIII low doses	compost, hydroculture; hanging plant; O: 20–25° C/68–77° F (for 4 weeks at 15° C/59° F).
	Anthurium scherzerianum hybrid flamingo flower	all year	○		✓	weekly: III–IX low doses	compost, hydroculture; O: 20–25° C/68–77° F, light, humid.
	Aphelandra squarrosa saffron spike, zebra plant	VI–X	○		✓	fortnightly: III–VIII	compost, hydroculture; O: 20–26° C/68–79° F.
●	*Begonia elatior* hybrid flowering begonia	all year	○			fortnightly	one year only; O: 18–24° C/64–75° F.
	Brunfelsia ☠	I–VIII	○ – ◐		✓	fortnightly: III–IX	compost, hydroculture; O: XI–I at 10–12° C/50–54° F.
●	*Cactaceae* genera/species of desert cacti	III–IX	☼ – ○			fortnightly: IV–X	mineral compost, cactus fertilizer O: 5–10° C/41–50° F, bright, dry.
	Camellia	X–III	○		✓	fortnightly: IV–VII azalea fertilizer	compost only; O: 6–10° C/43–50° F, bright, well-ventilated.
	Catharanthus roseus Madagascar periwinkle ☠	V–X	○			fortnightly: III–VIII	compost only; O: around 15° C/59° F, bright.
●	*Chrysanthemum* hybrids pot chrysanthemum	all year	○			weekly: III–X	compost, all year round; not over 18° C/64° F.
	Clerodendrum	III–X	○		✓	weekly: III–VIII	compost, hydroculture; hanging plant; O: XII–II at 12° C/54° F, bright, then warmer.
	Clivia miniata ☠	II–V	○			fortnightly: III–VII	compost, hydroculture; O: X–II at 8–10° C/46–50° F, almost dry.
	Columnea	depends on species	○ – ◐		✓	weekly: III–VIII low doses	compost, hydroculture; hanging plant; O: 30–40 days at 15° C/59° F, encourages flowers.
	Cyclamen persicum cyclamen	IX–IV	○ – ◐			before and during flowering: weekly	compost only; O: 15° C/59° F, airy.
	Cymbidium (orchids)	IX–II	☼ – ○		✓	every 4 weeks: III–IX orchid fertilizer	Orchid compost; V–VI: warm in daytime, night-time 16° C/61° F; O: daytime 20° C/68° F, night 16° C/61° F.
	Epiphyllum hybrids (leaf cacti)	V–VII	○ – ◐		✓	fortnightly: III–VIII cactus fertilizer	compost only; also hanging plant; O: 12–15° C/54–59° F, drier.
	Euphorbia milii crown of thorns ☠	X–III	☼ – ○			fortnightly: III–VIII cactus fertilizer	compost, hydroculture; O: 15–24° C/59–75° F, bright.
●	*Euphorbia pulcherrima* poinsettia	XI–II	○			weekly: VI–X	compost, hydroculture; O: up to 20° C/68° F.
	Exacum affine Arabian violet, Persian violet	VII–IX	○			fortnightly: V–VIII	annual or biennial
●	*Gardenia*	VII–X	○		✓	weekly: III–VIII low doses	compost, hydroculture; O: 15–18° C/59–64° F, bright, humid.
	Hatiora hybrids	III–V	○ – ◐		✓	every 4 weeks: V–VIII cactus fertilizer	compost only; also in hanging baskets; O: 8 weeks at 10° C/50° F, otherwise 18–25° C/64–77° F
	Hibiscus rosa-sinensis	III–X	☼ – ○			weekly: III–VIII	compost, hydroculture; O: around 15° C/59° F, bright, humid.
	Hippeastrum hybrids amaryllis ☠	I–IV	○		✓	weekly: III–VIII	from VIII, hardly any water; to XII at 15° C/59° F, when no foliage, pot bulb, warm, bright.

The symbols: ● the plant is easy to care for, suitable for beginners and offices. ☠ Warning: plants or parts of them are toxic.

Light: ☼ = full sunlight, south-facing window; ○ = bright, east- or west-facing window; ◐ = semi-shade, north-facing window; ⬤ = shade, small north-facing window.

	Name	Flowering time	Light	Watering	Humidity	Fertilizing	Further tips on care
	Hoya wax plant	V–X	☼ – ○	[medium watering]		fortnightly: III–VIII low doses	compost, hydroculture; hanging, climbing plant; O: 15–18° C/59–64° F, bright.
	Hydrangea macrophylla	III–VII	○ – ◐	[water a lot]		fortnightly: V–VIII azalea fertilizer	compost only; O: 4–8° C/39–46° F, dark, loss of leaves.
●	*Impatiens* busy lizzie	nearly all year round	○ – ◐	[medium watering]		weekly: III–IX	compost, hydroculture; also hanging plant; O: 18–25° C/64–77° F, bright.
●	*Jasminum* jasmine	VI–IX	○	[water a lot]		fortnightly: V–VIII	compost only; climbing plant; O: below 10° C/50° F, bright.
	Kalanchoë blossfeldiana flaming Katy	II–V	☼ – ○	[medium watering]		every 4 weeks: III–VIII cactus fertilizer	compost, hydroculture; O: 16–25° C/61–77° F, bright
●	*Kalanchoë manginii*	II–III	○	[medium watering]		every 4 weeks: III–VIII cactus fertilizer	compost only; hanging plant; O: 10–14° C/50–57° F, drier.
	Mandevilla ☠	V–X	○	[water a lot]	[humidity]	weekly: III–VIII	compost only; climbing plant; O: 15–24° C/59–75° F, bright, humid.
	Medinilla magnifica	IV–VII	○	[medium watering]	[humidity]	weekly: III–VIII	compost only; O: for 2 months at 16° C/61° F, otherwise always above 20° C/68° F, moist and warm.
	Miltonia, pansy orchid	VI–XI	○	[medium watering]	[humidity]	every 3 weeks: III–VII orchid fertilizer	orchid compost; O: daytime around 20° C/68° F, night 15–18° C/59–64° F, humid air.
	Nematanthus	VIII–III	○	[water sparingly]		fortnightly: III–VIII	compost only; hanging plant; O: 12–15° C/54–59° F, almost dry.
	Paphiopedilum hybrids slipper orchids	depends on variety	◐	[medium watering]	[humidity]	every 3 weeks: IV–IX orchid fertilizer	orchid compost; IX: 2–3 weeks cool at night, daytime sunny; O: 20–24° C/68–75° F.
●	*Passiflora* passion flower	VI–IX	☼ – ○	[water a lot]	[humidity]	weekly: III–VIII	compost, hydroculture; climbing plant; O: around 15° C/59° F, bright, airy.
	Pelargonium grandiflorum hybrids	all year round	☼ – ○	[water a lot]		weekly: III–VIII	compost only; O: 10–15° C/50–59° F, airy.
	Pentas lanceolata	IX–I	○	[medium watering]		fortnightly: III–VIII low doses	compost only; O: 12–15° C/54–59° F.
	Pericallis x *hybrida* cineraria	III–IV	○	[water a lot]	[humidity]	weekly: II–IV	annual
	Phalaenopsis hybrids	all year round	○	[medium watering]	[humidity]	fortnightly: V–VIII orchid fertilizer	compost, hydroculture; O: daytime 20–24° C/68–75° F, cooler at night; autumn 4–6 weeks at 16° C/61° F.
●	*Rhododendron* indoor azalea	XI–IV	○ – ◐	[water a lot]	[humidity]	fortnightly: V–VIII azalea fertilizer	compost only; O: from X about 5–10° C/41–50° F; buds appear at about 18° C/64° F.
	Saintpaulia ionantha hybrids African violet	all year round	○ – ◐	[medium watering]		weekly: III–VIII low doses	compost, hydroculture; O: 18–25° C/64–77° F, bright, humid air.
	Schlumbergera hybrids	XII–III	○ – ◐	[medium watering]	[humidity]	fortnightly: III–VIII cactus fertilizer	compost only; also in hanging baskets; O: 18–22° C/64–72° F, bright.
	Sinningia hybrids gloxinia	III–VIII	○	[medium watering]	[humidity]	weekly: III–VIII	after flowering, wait for leaves to retract. Overwinter the tuber in a dry place at 15° C/59° F.
	Stephanotis floribunda	VI–IX	○	[medium watering]	[humidity]	weekly: III–VIII	compost, hydroculture; climbing plant; O: 12–14° C/54–57° F, warmer when buds begin to form.
	Streptocarpus Cape primrose	V–IX	○ – ◐	[medium watering]	[humidity]	fortnightly: III–VIII	compost, hydroculture; O: 18–24° C/64–75° F, bright, humid air.
	Tillandsia (bromeliads)	depends on species	○	[humidity]	[humidity]	fortnightly: V–VIII low doses	tied to branches, epiphytic; O: grey species 10–15° C/50–59° F, green ones 20–26° C/68–79° F.
	Zantedeschia	III–VII	☼ – ○	[water a lot]		weekly: VIII–flowering	compost, hydroculture; after flowering, keep dry for 2 whole months. Repot, then water more.

Watering: [water a lot] = water a lot; [medium watering] = medium watering, keep the plant constantly moist; [water sparingly] = water sparingly, allow compost to dry off.
Humidity: [humidity] = medium or high humidity. Roman numerals = months. O = overwintering.

Foliage plants and their care

Caladias (Caladium hybrids) only display their splendid leaves from summer to autumn, then they die back into their tubers until the following year.

The very spectacular Coleus blumei.

Green means variety

Foliage houseplants originate from many different countries. A huge range of families can be found, including leafy bushes, woody shrubs and proper trees, held in check only by the dimensions of their pots.

Shades of green: Maranta.

There are upright, prostrate, climbing and hanging species, with large or small, soft or tough, single coloured or multi-coloured leaves. Naturally, such individuality calls for very different requirements as to care. Many of the plants' needs can be guessed at by looking at their leaves.

What the leaves tell us

Fleshy leaves: usually indicate that the plant is able to store moisture and can cope with a temporary lack of water and plenty of sun.
Variegated leaves: (white- or yellow-patterned foliage) contain less chlorophyll than green species and should be placed in brighter (but never sunny.) positions.
Large, soft leaves: should never be left in the sun or they will lose too much water through evaporation. They will always need plenty of humid air.
Leathery, tough leaves: are a feature of plants that can cope with plenty of light (but not sunlight) and which will survive a temporary shortage of water.

The variegated leaves of Epipremnum pinnatum.

The ribbed fern.

Indoor ferns

These are among the oldest plants in the world and they do not reproduce through flowers but through spores. Nearly all indoor ferns are natives of tropical rain forests, with evergreen fronds and similar requirements for care:

- no bright sunlight;
- keep warm from below, never allow cold draughts;
- high humidity. This is the reason most ferns do not thrive in the dry air of centrally heated rooms;
- soft, lukewarm water;
- a constant rate of moisture in the soil;
- no waterlogging.

A spreading Washingtonia.

Palms

These leafy beauties generally grow very slowly. A distinction is made between feathery palms with deeply indented fronds, such as *Chamaedorea elegans*, and fan palms with more rounded leaves, such as the *Washingtonia* species. The requirements for care are as follows:

- very bright position but never in bright sunlight;
- humid air; the tips of the leaves go brown in dry air;
- medium moist soil, but no waterlogging. Never water the "heart" of the palm, as it decays very easily;
- use tall, narrow pots when repotting.

Care at a glance

Name	Light	Watering	Humidity	Fertilizing	Further tips on care
Adiantum maidenhair fern	○–◐		✓	fortnightly: III–IX low doses	compost, hydroculture; O: as in summer, never below 18° C/64° F.
● *Aeonium* (succulent)	☼			fortnightly: V–VIII cactus fertilizer	compost only; O: almost dry, 10–16° C/50–61° F.
Ananas decorative pineapple (bromeliad)	☼–○			fortnightly: V–VIII	compost, hydroculture; soft water; O: 18–25° C/64–77° F.
Araucaria heterophylla Norfolk Island pine	○		✓	fortnightly: III–VIII low doses	compost, hydroculture; soft water; O: 5–15° C/41–59° F, a little drier.
● *Asparagus* ornamental asparagus ☠	○			weekly: III–VIII	compost, hydroculture; O: never below 12° C/54° F, dry.
● *Aspidistra elatior*	○–●			fortnightly: III–VIII	compost, hydroculture; O: never under 10° C/50° F, a little drier.
Asplenium nidus bird's nest fern	○–◐		✓	fortnightly: III–IX	compost, hydroculture, also epiphytic; O: 16–25° C/61–77° F; soft water.
Begonia foliage begonia	○		✓	fortnightly: III–IX	compost, hydroculture; soft water; O: 16–25° C/61–77° F.
Caladium	○–◐		✓	weekly: III–VII	compost, hydroculture; O: tubers dry at 18° C/64° F.
Calathea	○–◐		✓	fortnightly: III–VIII	compost, hydroculture; O: 16–22° C/61–72° F.
● *Chlorophytum comosum* spider plant, St Bernard's lily	○–◐		✓	weekly: III–VIII	compost, hydroculture, also hanging plant; O: 10–22° C/50–72° F.
● *Cissus*	○–◐			weekly: III–VIII	compost, hydroculture, climbing, hanging plant; O: 16–24° C/61–75° F.
Cocos nucifera coconut palm	○		✓	weekly: IV–IX low doses	compost, hydroculture; O: 18–24° C/64–75° F.
Codiaeum ☠	○		✓	weekly: III–VIII low doses	compost, hydroculture; O: 16–24° C/61–75° F.
● *Coleus blumei* hybrids	☼			fortnightly: III–VIII	compost, hydroculture; O: 13–24° C/55–75° F.
Cordyline fruticosa	○		✓	fortnightly: III–VIII	compost, hydroculture; O: 16–24° C/61–75° F.
● *Crassula arborescens* (succulent)	☼–○			every 4 weeks: V–VIII	compost, hydroculture; O: around 10° C/50° F, dry.
● *Cyperus*	○		✓	fortnightly: I–VIII	compost, hydroculture; O: 15–24° C/59–75° F.
Dieffenbachia ☠	○–◐		✓	weekly: III–VIII low doses	compost, hydroculture; O: 16–24° C/61–75° F.
● *Dracaena* dragon plant, ribbon plant	○–◐		✓	fortnightly: III–VIII	compost, hydroculture; O: 18–25° C/64–77° F.
● *Echeveria* (succulent)	☼			fortnightly: V–VIII cactus fertilizer	compost only; O:13–16° C/55–61° F, a little drier.
● *Epipremnum pinnatum*	○–◐			weekly: III–VIII	compost, hydroculture; hanging plant; O: 16–24° C/61–75° F.
x *Fatshedera lizei* ☠	☼–○		✓	fortnightly: III–VIII	compost, hydroculture; O: 10–18° C/50–64° F, a little drier.
● *Ficus* rubber tree, *Ficus benjamina* and others	○		✓	fortnightly: III–VIII	compost, hydroculture; some species are hanging plants; O: 18–25° C/64–77° F.

The symbols: ● the plant is easy to care for, suitable for beginners and offices. ☠ Warning: plants or parts of them are toxic.
Light: ☼ = full sunlight, south-facing window; ○ = bright, east- or west-facing window; ◐ = semi-shade, north-facing window; ● = shade, small north-facing window.

Name		Light	Watering	Humidity	Fertilizing	Further tips on care
Fittonia albivenis Verschaffeltii Group		○–●	medium	medium or high	fortnightly: IV–X	compost, hydroculture; O: 18–25° C/64–77° .
Hedera ivy	☠	○–◐	medium	medium or high	weekly: II–VIII low doses	compost, hydroculture; climbing and hanging plant; O: not below 15° C/59° F.
Howea		○–◐	medium	medium or high	weekly: III–IX low doses	compost, hydroculture; O: 18–25° C/64–77° F.
Maranta		○	a lot	medium or high	fortnightly: IV–VIII low doses	compost, hydroculture; O: 18–24° C/64–75° F, a little drier.
Monstera deliciosa Swiss cheese plant		○	medium	medium or high	fortnightly: III–VIII low doses	compost, hydroculture; climbing plant; O: 18–22° C/64–72° F, humid air.
Myrtus communis myrtle		☼–○	a lot	medium or high	weekly: III–VIII	compost only; O: 6–10° C/43–50° F, bright, dry.
Nephrolepis exaltata ladder fern		○–◐	medium	medium or high	fortnightly: III–IX low doses	compost, hydroculture O: 18–25° C/64–77° F, humid air.
Pachypodium Madagascar palm	☠	☼	medium		every 4 weeks: V–VIII cactus fertilizer	compost, hydroculture; O: 18–25° C/64–77° F.
Pelargonium foliage and scented pelargoniums		☼–○	a lot		weekly: III–VIII	compost only; O: 10–12° C/50–54° F, bright and dry.
Peperomia dwarf pepper		○	sparingly	medium or high	every 3 weeks: IV–IX	compost, hydroculture; some species are also suitable for hanging baskets; O: 15–22° C/59–72° F.
Philodendron		○–◐	medium	medium or high	fortnightly: III–VIII	compost, hydroculture; some climbing; O: 18–26° C/64–79° F.
Platycerium staghorn fern		○–◐	medium	medium or high	fortnightly: III–IX	compost or epiphytic; also hanging plant; O: 18–25° C/64–77° F.
Pogonatherum paniceum indoor bamboo		○	a lot	medium or high	every 3 weeks: III–VIII	compost only; O: 15–24° C/59–75° F.
Radermachera sinica		○	medium	medium or high	every 3 weeks: III–VIII	compost only; O: around 15° C/59° F.
Rhoicissus capensis		○–◐	sparingly		fortnightly: V–VIII	compost, hydroculture; climbing plant; O: 10–16° C/50–61° F.
Sansevieria trifasciata mother-in-law's tongue		☼–◐	sparingly		every 3 weeks: III–VIII	compost, hydroculture; O: 15–24° C/59–75° F.
Saxifraga stolonifera saxifrage		○–◐	sparingly		weekly: III–VIII	compost, hydroculture; hanging plant; O: 15–24° C/59–75° F.
Schefflera		○–◐	sparingly	medium or high	fortnightly: III–VIII	compost, hydroculture; O: 16–24° C/61–75° F.
Sedum		☼–○	sparingly		every 4 weeks: IV–VIII cactus fertilizer	compost only; some species are also suitable for hanging baskets; O: 5–10° C/41–50° F.
Sparrmannia africana African hemp		○	a lot	medium or high	weekly: III–VIII	compost, hydroculture; O: 10–15° C/50–59° F, a little drier,
Tetrastigma voinierianum		○–◐	medium		weekly: III–VIII	compost only; climbing plant; O: 10–24° C/50–75° F.
Tolmiea menziesii youth on age		○–◐	a lot		fortnightly: III–VIII	compost only; also for hanging baskets; O: 5–10° C/41–50° F.
Tradescantia		○	medium		fortnightly: III–VIII	compost, hydroculture; hanging plant; O: 10–24° C/50–75° F.
Yucca		☼–○	medium		every 3 weeks: III–VIII	compost, hydroculture; O: 5–10° C/41–50° F, a litle drier.

Watering: (a lot) = water a lot; (medium) = medium watering, keep the plant constantly moist; (sparingly) = water sparingly, allow compost to dry off.
Humidity: (medium or high) = medium or high humidity. Roman numerals = months. O = overwintering.

The vital requirements of plants

Houseplants will thrive and flourish if their basic requirements are adequately met. This means supplying everything they need to live, at the right time and in the right amounts. The requirements for growth are:

- water (see watering, p. 25);
- air and humidity (see humidity, p. 32);
- nutrients (see fertilizing, p. 37 or repotting, p. 45);
- temperature, i.e. warmth and coolness at the right times (see growth cycle, p. 6);
- light (see light and plant care, p. 18).

My tip: Houseplants will do best if all these factors are combined correctly. Stick to the following general rules.

Water

- Water supports the metabolic processes of plants. Plants comprise 90% water, which evaporates through tiny openings that are usually situated on the undersides of the leaves. This creates a lack of moisture in the plant, which, in turn, creates a suction effect and causes the plant to draw water up through its roots.
- Water carries dissolved nutrients, gathered through the roots from the soil.
- Water not only conducts nutrients to the plant but also washes out the waste products of metabolic processes.
- Water helps the plant to cope with high temperatures. When it is very hot, the water evaporates and this provides an auto-cooling system for the plant. Without this facility, the plant would die in intense sunlight.
- Water keeps the plant tissues firm. If there is a lack of water, the cells become flabby. We can recognize this by the limp and faded appearance of the plant.

General rules

1. Never water too much, as waterlogging will rapidly lead to decaying roots and thus prevent nutrients from reaching the plant.
2. When temperatures are low or humidity is high, water less as the plant is losing less water through evaporation than when the air is dry.
3. If temperatures are high and the air is dry, water more and frequently as the plant loses water through evaporation.

Air

Plants require air to breathe (see illustration, p. 7) and to stay healthy. Stagnant air, which is created when plants are left standing too close together, or intense sunlight which penetrates a south-facing window (heat accumulation), will soon render plants susceptible to infestation by pests.
The plants also take in moisture with the air. The requirements of tropical plants are often above 60% humidity.

General rules:

1. Plant care also involves airing the plant and providing humid air.
2. The higher the temperature is in a room, the more humidity is required by the plants.
3. Draughts are harmful to all houseplants. Particularly in winter, protect your plants from draughts whenever you air the room.
4. Stale air or air laden with harmful substances (for example, cigarette smoke) is bad for plants and may cause leaves, flowers and buds to drop off.

Nourishment

As a rule, nutrients are delivered to the plant through the soil or compost or by fertilizers.
A distinction is made between the main nutrients (see table, p. 39) and trace elements (see p. 38).
Individual houseplants have very different nutritional requirements. Some just seem to gobble up nutrients, while others use only very small amounts (for example, cacti and orchids). The size of the plant also determines the amount of fertilizer it needs. Large, fast-growing plants will require more nutrients than young plants.

General rules:

1. Always fertilize plants whenever there is more light, warmth or increased watering during the main growth phase.
2. Never fertilize plants during times of dormancy, when it is cool, there is less light and watering is at a minimum.
3. Typical symptoms of a lack of nutrients can be alleviated very fast with the use of liquid fertilizers (see p. 43) or with leaf fertilizer that is sprayed on.
4. Even regular fertilizing will not replace necessary repotting (see p. 45).
5. Houseplants that are grown in hydroculture or an alternative medium, such as clay pellets (Hortag), will require special fertilizers that are intended for use with this kind of medium (see p. 42).

Epiphytes – such as this nest fern – colonize trees and require semi-shade as well as high humidity.

Temperature

Plants slow their metabolic rate when temperatures drop, while warmth causes an increase in growth as well as encouraging the absorption of nutrients.

With respect to temperature, most houseplants have similar requirements to humans, which is around 16–22° C/61–72° F – but, in keeping with prevailing conditions in their countries of origin, they generally prefer lower temperatures at night. Orchids, in particular, require a drop in temperature at night in order to produce flowers.

One factor which nearly always has a harmful effect on tropical plants is a low temperature near the ground. During the winter, and in transition from one season to another, the temperature around a plant container may often sink faster than the room temperature if the plant is positioned on a cold, badly insulated windowsill or placed in front of a draughty balcony door. In such cases, the plant should be moved to another position or you should provide some kind of insulation, such as polystyrene sheets or cork mats.

General rules

1. A rest phase always requires a drop in temperature. The plants should hardly be watered at all and should not be fertilized.
2. Beware of cold around the base of the plant. Tropical plants are particularly sensitive, as are all plants grown in hydroculture as they are not protected from the cold by soil.
3. Cold floors/windowsills etc., combined with waterlogging, are lethal for all houseplants.

Light and plant care

All parts of plants that grow above ground reach towards the light, especially flowers and leaves. It is quite different for the underground parts of plants – roots always grow away from the light.

My tip: Once they have developed buds, do not turn plants that are positioned on a windowsill.

Light symbols

Light is measured in lux. When you buy a houseplant, you will often find it accompanied by a little card or tag with instant information represented by small care symbols. Usually, these include the light requirements of the plant, perhaps with the following symbols:

= full sunlight. A position in a south-facing window or outside. The light intensity factor is above 2000 lux.

= bright. An east- or west-facing window, as well as south-east and south-west positions with sunlight shining in for several hours of the day but no intense midday sun. On average, 1500–2000 lux.

= semi-shady. Unshaded, north-facing windows as well as north-west and north-east positions which never receive direct sunlight but are not obscured by any objects. On average, 1000 lux.

= shady. Small or shaded north-, north-west- and north-east-facing positions as well as positions inside a room up to 2 m (80 in) away from the window. Light intensity factor below 1000 lux.

My tip: These factors may deviate considerably upwards or downwards. You can measure the conditions at your window with a luxmeter, which functions like a light meter.

Is the light OK?

Plants soon show whether they are happy or not with the existing light conditions. Light is such an important part of their lives that it has a direct effect on their shape and appearance. On average, it is important for plants to receive twelve to sixteen hours of light per day. If it receives the ***correct amount of light***, a plant will grow compact and dense.

- The shoots will be robust, the spaces between branches and leaves small.
- The flowers will be numerous and a good colour.
- Coloured or variegated (white- or yellow-patterned) leaves will be particularly well marked.

If there is ***not enough light***, the plants will only grow towards the source of light.

- Their shoots will grow lanky (particularly if the plant is kept warm and watered regularly), which makes it become "leggy" so that the spaces between branches and leaves will greatly increase (see first aid, p. 58).
- The leaves will look untypical and be small and yellowish; coloured or variegated foliage turns green.
- Flowers are hardly ever produced.

If there is ***too much light***, plants respond rather like we do – they suffer sunburn. At first the plant goes limp, then yellow, later brown spots appear on the leaves (see first aid, p. 58).

South-facing windows

This position will receive full sunlight from morning to afternoon.

- During the winter, when there is much less light, this is a good position for all plants which prefer light or semi-shade at other times of the year.
- Be careful in the summer. From the first month of spring right through to autumn, it will become so hot that only sun-loving plants, such as cacti, succulents and large container plants, can cope.

Tips for plants in a south-facing window:

- You can use a south-facing window for plants all year round if you do not place them directly in the window but, rather, near the window, so that they are not exposed to the rays of the sun.
- You can stand all light-loving plants on a south-facing windowsill as long as you provide shade on sunny days, both in summer and in the winter. For example, half close the shutters or blinds, or place paper or shading foil between the glass and the plants.
- Alternative: During the winter, move plants from an east/west-facing window to this position. From the first month of spring, move them back to their less-exposed window seats.
- From spring to autumn, it is the turn of the "sun worshippers". Later, they can be moved to cool, bright winter quarters to enjoy their rest period.

Generally speaking, during the summer you should move all plants as far away from the windowpane as possible so that they cannot get burnt.

- In addition, water and air them daily so that no accumulation of heat takes place behind the windowpane.

East- and west-facing windows
East-facing positions receive soft morning light and west-facing positions the mellow evening light. Both windows enable plants to avoid the intense burning sunlight of midday but they will still receive enough light for most of your houseplants to thrive there – for example, most foliage plants, particularly those with coloured or variegated leaves, and numerous flowering plants, even orchids.

Tips for plants in east- or west-facing windows:

● In the case of south-east- or south-west-facing positions, provide shade at midday to filter out the harmful rays of the sun.

● During the winter, move plants from a north-facing window to one of these positions so that they will receive enough light.

North-facing windows
This position receives the least amount of light and is not suitable for most plants. Nevertheless, a wonderful assortment of plants can be kept here, particularly if the room is always kept at the same pleasant temperature all year round. You can grow all tropical rain forest plants here, most of which are characterized by attractive leaf shapes and markings – for example, *Maranta*, ferns and members of the Araceae family such as *Alocasia*, *Philodendron* and *Dieffenbachia*.

Tips for plants in north-facing windows:

● Coloured- or variegated-leaved plants may suffer from lack of light during the winter. If they start to lose their markings and turn green, it is a good idea to move the plants to an east- or west-facing window or make temporary use of a plant lamp to alleviate the problem.

Light intensity decreasing from left to right in a room

Right beside the window the plants will receive the full amount of available light, about 100%.

1 m (40 in) away from the window the plants receive about 80–50% of the light intensity in the window.

1.5 m (60 in) from the window the amount of light has dropped to 50–25%.

2 m (80 in) from the window is often the point at which artificial light will be necessary.

● Draughty, north-facing windows must be insulated as tropical rain forest plants are particularly sensitive to "cold feet". Root rot and falling leaves are often the consequence.

● If the plants are placed on a cold windowsill made of stone during the winter, they should be insulated through the use of warming mats, polystyrene sheets or humidifier dishes (see p. 35).

What reduces the intensity of light?
The amount of light in a room can be reduced by various factors:

● the size of the window;

● curtains – even light-coloured blinds will considerably reduce the amount of light penetrating the room;

● the position of the room;

● the immediate surroundings of the building; a large tree growing in front of a window will cast a large shadow;

● the seasons; plants receive more light in the summer than in the winter.

Pests and diseases

The wrong position and mistakes in care are the main causes of infestation by pests or disease.

Evil number one: Much suffering is caused when houseplants are in positions where they are unable to thrive.
Prevention: Make a point of considering the light and temperature requirements, as well as the growth and rest phases, of the plant.

Evil number two: Most plants are watered too much. If their roots stand in water for long periods, they will no longer be able to breathe and will begin to rot. As a result, the plant can no longer absorb water or nutrients in sufficient amounts and will gradually starve to death.
Prevention: Water regularly but sparingly.

Evil number three: If houseplants receive too many or too few nutrients, they will rapidly fall prey to pests such as aphids, spider mites or scale insects.
Prevention: Fertilize regularly but sparingly.

Evil number four: Overwintering in a position that is too warm, with arid air, encourages infestation by thrips, spider mites and white fly.
Prevention: Allow the temperature to drop in winter and make sure that warm rooms contain enough humidity.

Evil number five: Stale, polluted air or air that is too humid encourages fungal disease.
Prevention: Air the room regularly; do not place the plants too close together and do not spray or water the leaves.

Aphids
Symptoms: green or blackish-brown insects on young shoots, buds or leaves; sticky, deformed leaves.
Remedy: see pp. 22–3 – lacewings (*Chrysopa vulgaris*), gall midges, agents containing pyrethrum, tobacco brew.

Sooty mould
Symptoms: a sticky, black layer on leaves. Mould that grows on the sticky secretions of aphids.
Remedy: remove very badly affected leaves; wash off mildly affected leaves with lukewarm water.

White fly
Symptoms: approximately 2 mm ($^1/_{16}$ in) long, white flies with wings shaped like roof tiles, which fly up immediately the plant is touched. Their larvae are yellowish-green. Flies and larvae sit on the undersides of the leaves and suck the sap of the plant, depositing sticky honeydew which, in turn, encourages infestation with sooty mould. The leaves become spotted with yellow marks and eventually wilt. Infestation is encouraged by warm, dry air.
Remedy: see pp. 22–3 – spray with warm water or use ichneumon flies, sticky fly catcher cards or agents containing pyrethrum. Prevent by providing high humidity.

Thrips

Symptoms: 1mm ($^{1}/_{32}$ in) long, fringed-wing insects, striped yellow and black. They suck the sap of leaves and flowers. The first signs are whitish dots all over the leaves, along with tiny black spots of excrement. Later, when infestation is very heavy, the undersides of the leaves turn silvery-white.

Infestation is encouraged by dry, warm air.
Remedy: see pp. 22–3 – spray the plant with lukewarm water or use sticky fly catcher cards or agents containing pyrethrum. Prevent by providing high humidity.

Spider mites

Houseplants are often attacked by the common red spider mite.
Symptoms: the red mites, which are related to spiders, are only about $^{1}/_{2}$ mm ($^{1}/_{64}$ in) long and difficult to see with the naked eye. Signs of infestation: the uppersides of the leaves show tiny whitish spots. As infestation progresses, the dots merge to form larger marks and gossamer-fine webs appear on the undersides of the leaves and in the leaf axils.
Remedy: see pp. 22–3 – fast action is required. Spray the plant frequently with lukewarm water. Employ robber mites *(Amblyseius)*, a plant sauna or special preparations for use against spider mites. Prevent by providing high humidity and correct care. Spider mites are typical parasites on weakened plants.

Scale insects

There are several different species, all of which are difficult to control.
Symptoms: brown scales, which are immobile mature adults. The younger insects are lighter and more mobile. These pests attack the shoots and leaves and suck the sap from the main veins on the undersides of leaves. They also secrete a very sticky honeydew, which rapidly encourages infestation with sooty mould (see p. 20).
Remedy: see pp. 22–3 – fast action is required. Scratch off the scale insects or paint them with a solution of detergent and methylated spirit. Hard-leafed plants can be sprayed with tar oil but soft-leafed plants will not respond well to this.
My tip: Infestation by the closely related mealy bug produces very similar symptoms, although these pests can be distinguished by the appearance of cotton-wool-like shapes instead of scales. Use the same remedies as for scale insects.

Mildew

Fungal disease.
Symptoms: genuine mildew manifests itself as a whitish-grey, flour-like film on the uppersides and undersides of the leaves as well as on shoots, flowers and seeds. False mildew only appears on the undersides of leaves. The fungus penetrates the plant and spreads inside it.
Remedy: see pp. 22–3 – infested plant parts should be removed and destroyed. Lecithin preparations or chemical fungicides can be used.
My tip: Some plants are particularly susceptible to infestation by mildew, such as hydrangea, *Kalanchoë*, African violets, *Rhoicissus capensis* and roses.

Protection and first aid

Houseplants will thrive and grow into robust specimens if they are given the right position and cared for properly. If there are occasional problems, the most important thing is to deal with them as early on as possible.

Regular plant checks are part of a proper programme of care and are not an arduous task. During regular watering, take a look at your plants. Look closely at the shoot tips and buds as well the upper- and undersides of the leaves.

What to do when problems arise: Houseplants can become infested with pests and fungal, viral and bacterial diseases.

There are remedies to use against pests and fungal infections. The earlier you discover the problem, the better your chances of successful control.

Unfortunately, bacterial and viral diseases are a different matter as there are no real cures. Fortunately, plants are very rarely attacked by them. If they should occur, however, the correct procedure is to destroy the infested plant immediately, but do not put the plant on a compost heap as this may cause the problem to spread to other plants.

My tip: Isolate any houseplants that have become infested with pests or fungal diseases so that the problem cannot spread to other plants. If the plant is badly affected, you should consider whether the cost and time involved in employing toxic agents are really warranted, or whether it would be better to replace the plant with a new one.

Alternative methods of control

Plant sauna
High humidity is a good remedy for spider mites. Water the plant well, then cover it with a transparent plastic bag tied around the pot to create an air-tight "bubble". Leave the plant like this for a few days. Warning: Soft-leaved plants may begin to decay.

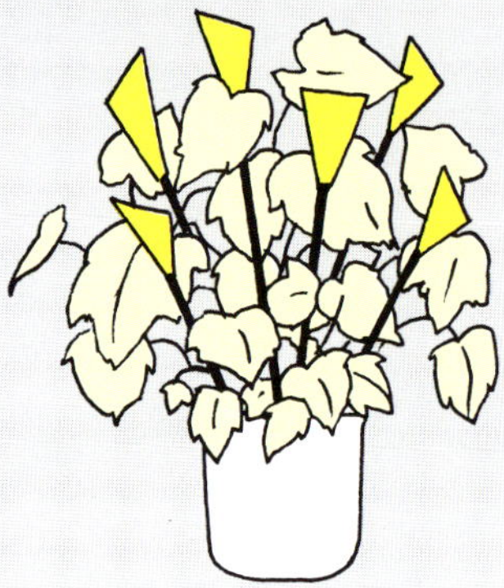

Bio friendly fly catchers
These sticky cards are a useful way of controlling white fly, *Liriomyza, Sciaridae* and thrips. Push the cards into the soil. The pests are attracted by the bright colour and then become stuck to the substance with which the card is coated.

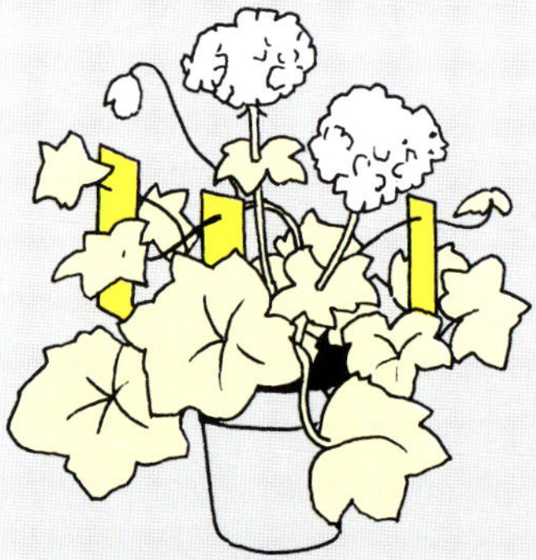

Useful insects
The eggs of insects that prey on pests are stuck on little cards which can be hung among the leaves of the affected plant until they hatch.

Alternative sprays
Fill a plant misting bottle with the agent and spray the plant. Repeat at intervals of several days (recipes, see p. 23).

Mechanical control
The earlier you discover an infestation, the less damage will have been done so that matters can often be put right easily. For example, by:
- cutting off infested or diseased parts of the plant;
- scraping off or spraying the pests;
- submerging the above-ground parts of the plant in a lukewarm detergent solution.

Biological measures
(see table, left)
Useful insects, which are the natural enemies of the pests, can be employed. Their eggs, which are attached to leaves or to a small piece of card, can be obtained through the gardening trade. They are hung among the leaves of the plant and become effective as soon as the larvae emerge from the eggs (which means there is a slight delay).
- for aphids, use damsel flies and predatory gall midges;
- for white fly, use ichneumon flies;
- for spider mites, use robber mites (*Amblyseius*);
- for mealy bugs, use Australian ladybirds (*Cryptolaemus montrouzieri*)
- for *Sciaridae,* use nematodes.

Sticky yellow cards attract white fly, *Liriomyza, Sciaridae*, thrips and other insects with their bright colour. The insects then stick fast to the substance that coats the cards.
Agents containing pyrethrum are sprayed on the affected plants. This substance is effective against all biting, sucking insects, in particular, white fly and aphids. These biological agents are derived from the flowers of a species of chrysanthemum and are not harmful to bees.
Never employ an agent containing pyrethrum if you have an open cut or wound, as the substance may enter your bloodstream and cause poisoning. Never use it in a room containing an aquarium.
Agents containing oil, for example, paraffin or tar oil, will clog up the tracheae of insects so that they suffocate. These agents are particularly good against mealy bugs, scale insects and spider mites but, just like sprays that make leaves shine, they are only tolerated by hard-leaved plants.
Agents containing lecithin are sprayed on the leaves to combat fungi that cause mildew.
Detergent-spirit solutions are easy to make up and are particularly successful against mealy bugs and scale insects.
Dissolve 1 tbsp soft soap in 1 litre (1¾ pt) lukewarm water and then add 1 tbsp methylated spirits. Spray the plant with the solution or dab it on to infested patches.
Tobacco brew is a good remedy for scale insects.
Remove the tobacco from about two cigarettes and soak it in ½ litre (¾ pt) water for about eight hours, then strain it. This undiluted solution can be sprayed straight on to the plants.
Warning: This solution is highly toxic. Use it only on robust plants. Keep it away from children and pets.

Chemical agents
Use these only if all other methods have failed.
- Insecticides kill insects and may be sprayed, poured or sprinkled on the soil or compost, or pushed into the compost in the form of small sticks.
- Acaricides destroy mites.
- Fungicides are effective against fungal infections.

Take care when using plant protection agents

- Do not use highly toxic agents.
- Follow the instructions for use and dosage meticulously. Keep to the prescribed intervals for spraying, so that succeeding generations of the pest are destroyed at the same time.
- To protect the environment, do not use any sprays containing CFCs.
- Only use the spray outside.
- Wear gloves and a mask to avoid inhaling the spray.
- Never eat, drink or smoke while handling plant protection agents.
- Always store plant protection agents in their original packaging, out of reach of children and pets and locked away.
- Do not store remains of any agents. The effectiveness of these preparations dissipates rapidly. Do not discard any surplus in ordinary household refuse but take it along to a special collection point for environmentally sensitive waste.

Water is essential for plants. Houseplants receive water through spraying or watering. If you happen to forget occasionally, a good soak will help.

Watering

It is an unfortunate truth that most houseplants do not die of thirst but are watered to death. The following pages will explain the right way to water houseplants. Arid, centrally heated rooms also require some attention.

Watering

In their natural state, plants receive all the moisture they need from rain, dew, mist or snow and have spent thousands of years adapting to the water supply that is available where they grow. Most plants draw up the greater part of the moisture they require through their roots: some even live on dew which they absorb through their leaf scales (e.g. *Tillandsia*).
In the artificial environment of a room, plants require proper care that will, as far as possible, replicate the conditions they are used to in the wild. Watering is a vital part of good care. In order to water properly, you must take various factors into consideration, giving each plant:

- the right kind of water;
- at the right time;
- in the right quantities.

Water hardness

Very soft water up to 3.19 deg. Clark	Not suitable for watering plants when pure. Can be mixed with harder mains water to make it less soft.
Soft water 3.20–10 deg. Clark	Best for watering.
Medium-hard water 11–20 deg. Clark	Too hard for many plants (see table, p. 28). ● Many plants can still manage on 11–13 degrees Clark if the water has been allowed to stand overnight. This causes some of the lime to be removed (in the form of a residue) and the water becomes slightly softer. ● At 13–20 degrees Clark, boil the water and allow it to cool. Large quantities of lime will be removed in the form of lime deposits in the vessel used for boiling and the water becomes softer.
Hard water 21–38 deg. Clark Very hard water above 38 deg. Clark	Definitely needs softening. The best way is to obtain softening agents from the gardening trade or use filter watering cans which are able to produce specially soft water for watering plants (see p. 27).

Hard or soft water

The quality of the water used is more important than many people know. Every indoor gardener should give some thought to the kind of mains water they have before buying any plant to take home. It is important to know that the water will not be too hard and does not, therefore, have a high lime content. Few plants can cope with very hard water for a long time.

How to assess the hardness of your mains water: The hardness of the water is measured in degrees Clark and depends on the content of certain mineral salts which are dissolved in it, foremost among them being magnesium and calcium compounds. These substances are needed in small quantities by most plants. If they are present in too great a concentration, however, they may hinder the absorption of nutrients and interfere with the metabolic processes of the plant.

What makes the water hard? The total hardness of water comprises the carbonate hardness (CH) and the non-carbonate hardness (NCH).

- Carbonate hardness (CH) is the main element of the total hardness and is decisive for the care of plants. It is also called temporary hardness as it can be altered relatively simply and quickly by boiling the mains water. The carbonate hardness in water used for watering houseplants should, if possible, not exceed 10 CH as, otherwise, the soil or compost in which the plant is growing will become increasingly alkaline, which means that the pH factor will rise (see p. 28). In turn, this means that the plant will have difficulty in absorbing some of the nutrients and trace elements. In spite of plenty of fertilizing, the plant will suffer from mineral deficiency (chlorosis), the leaves will turn yellow and only the veins will remain green.
- Non-carbonate hardness (NCH) cannot be removed by boiling the water and is, therefore, called permanent hardness. It is based on sulphate compounds of calcium and magnesium and is usually unimportant in respect of plant care.

How to measure the hardness of your mains water
Mains water may show considerable regional variations in hardness. You can find out about your own particular values by enquiring at your regional or local water authority.
If, however, you wish to make a test yourself, you can acquire reagents from an aquarium supplier to determine either the total hardness or just the carbonate hardness. There is also an old gardening trick for roughly determining the hardness of water. If chalky rings appear on the leaves of sclerophyllous plants that you have sprayed with water, then the water is medium hard or very hard and should definitely be softened.

Be careful with very soft or distilled water
Neither very soft water (below 3.19 degrees Clark) nor distilled water should be used for watering plants. The nutrients that are lacking in the water cannot be replaced by fertilizer. Water from ion exchange devices that are regenerated with salt should never be used for watering plants either as this would be harmful for them. Desalinated water obtained by these methods can, however, be mixed with mains water to make it softer.
My tip: In most ordinary households there will often be a supply of water that can be used for plants because it contains little lime and may even contain some valuable nutrients, for example, cooled water left over from boiling potatoes or water used for cooking green vegetables.

How to soften water for plants

Softening agents
These can be obtained in powder or liquid form. Mix with water and allow this to stand for six to twelve hours so that the lime can accumulate at the bottom of the vessel. Then either pass the liquid through a coffee filter or pour off the softened water, leaving the residue behind.
My tip: This is very useful for anyone needing lots of water.

Filter watering cans
Cans specially made for watering houseplants can be obtained in the gardening trade. The filter cartridge, which contains ion exchange substances, will have to be changed regularly. This filter softens the water and filters out harmful substances.
My tip: This is practical if only small amounts of water are required.

Peat sack
This is an old home remedy. Fill a small sack with 500 g (17½ oz) dry peat and suspend it overnight in a bucket containing 10 litres (17½ pt) water. Change the peat after it has been used three times.
My tip: Only use this method if you have no other alternative as the overextraction of peat is a threat to the natural environment.

Mains water or rain water?
As a rule, ***mains water*** is harder than rain water and, in many cases, also contains chlorine. It will often have to be treated before it can be used for watering plants.
Rain water is not available to every indoor gardener and the quality of some rain water is not always very good. Depending on where you live, you may not be able to collect rain water. People living in country areas or in an environment that is unpolluted should be able to collect it without problems. If you live in an area that is polluted by industrial fumes or other air pollutants, you may not wish to use rain water for your precious plants. Nevertheless, most of the time it is plant-friendly, soft and at the right temperature. However, do remember the following rules:

- Do not collect rain water until it has been raining for half an hour to an hour and the majority of dirt particles and other harmful substances have been washed from the air.
- If you suspect your rain water may be too acid, you can obtain test strips and indicators for checking the pH factor in the gardening trade or at aquarium retailers.

The degree of acidity (pH factor)

The degree of acidity is measured in pH values on a scale from 0–14; the value 7 indicates a neutral reaction.

- The ideal pH value for water for houseplants is around 5.5 to 6. Most plants do best at these pH values.
- If the pH value is below 5, the water will be too acid for most plants and should not be used for watering.
- A pH value of more than 7.5 can be lowered by softening the water (see table, p. 27).

What can be done about harmful substances in the water?

Both mains water and rain water may contain substances that are harmful to plants.
In rain water, ***heavy metal compounds*** containing cadmium, copper and lead are toxins which can interfere with the metabolism of plants.

- Remedy: special filters for treating water (see table, p. 27). The filter cartridges containing special ion exchangers have to be changed regularly and can be taken back to the retailer for recycling.

Chlorine and substances forming chlorine compounds interfere with the growth of plants and affect their health. Water used for plants should contain no more than 50 mg per litre ($1^3/_4$ pt).

- Remedy: Allow water to stand overnight as the chlorine will then disperse. Information about the chlorine content of mains water can also be obtained from your local water authority.

Houseplants that require soft water

- flamingo plant (*Anthurium*)
- zebra plant (*Aphelandra*)
- *Begonia*
- *Camellia*
- *Dieffenbachia*
- *Fittonia*
- *Gardenia*
- *Hydrangea*
- *Ixora*
- jasmine (*Jasminum*)
- South Sea myrtle (*Leptospermum*)
- *Mandevilla*
- *Maranta*
- *Medinilla*
- myrtle (*Myrtus*)
- *Pentas*
- indoor azalea (*Rhododendron*)
- *Schefflera*

as well as indoor ferns and palms, bromeliads and orchids.

The right tools

Many houseplants cannot cope with water or moisture on their leaves and flowers. With very few exceptions, it is best to water the compost or soil. The following implements are best suited for this purpose.
Watering cans with long, narrow spouts, as the compost can be reached directly, even through bushy plants.

My tip: Watering cans with a spray device are unsuitable for houseplants as, although they make the water soft, they distribute it too widely.

Filter watering cans with ion exchangers are particularly practical but do be careful when buying one as there are two kinds: those that prepare water for the household (as for coffee, tea and electric steam irons) and those that are specially designed to produce softened water for houseplants.
Pumping cans, with a long, curved spout, are eminently suitable for watering hanging baskets and hanging arrangements. The water is pumped up from the bottle-shaped can and out through the spout by pressure.

My tip: Look after your watering can. Limestone, bacteria and other residue may be deposited in a watering can. I recommend cleaning the can thoroughly, including the inside, once a week under running water.

Use only soft water for orchids and definitely avoid waterlogging. Provide high humidity.

The correct way to water

It is well worth finding out how often, and in what way, each type of houseplant prefers to be watered.

When to water

- If you can no longer feel any moisture when you push your finger 1–2 cm (½–¾ in) into the soil.
- If tapping a clay pot yields a high-pitched tone. If the soil is well moistened right through, the tapping will sound muffled.

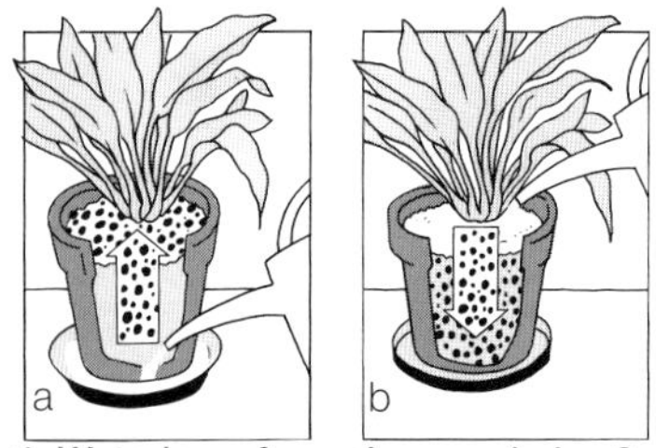

1. Watering – from above or below?
a) Constant watering from below carries water and nutrients upwards.
b) Vigorous watering from the top will distribute water and nutrients evenly in the pot.

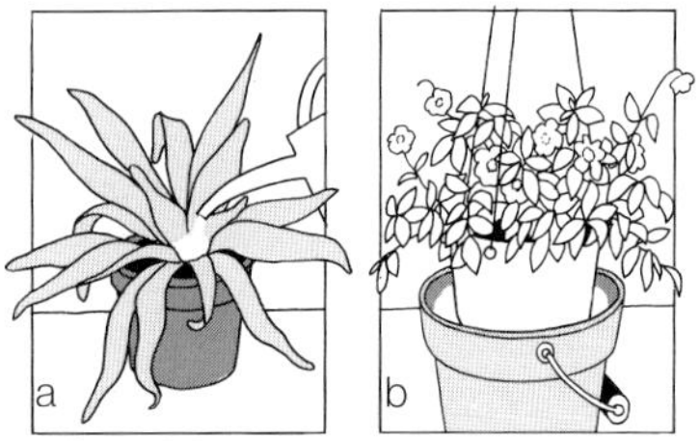

2. Special watering methods
a) Water the funnels of bromeliads.
b) When giving plants a "bath", keep them submerged until no more air bubbles rise up. Then allow the plant to drip dry.

- It is absolutely essential if the soil has shrunk away from the edges of the pot and the plant is looking limp.

My tip: You have given your plant too much water if clay pots are constantly moist or are coated with a layer of green algae on the outside. Moisture meters are very useful (see illustration 3). They are pushed into the soil in the pot.

Watering methods

Watering from below (see illustration 1a) is recommended for plants with sensitive tubers, stalks or leaves, such as cyclamen, African violets or gloxinia. Allow water to accumulate in the saucer under the pot for no longer than half an hour, after which any surplus should be poured away so that the roots do not decay.
The disadvantage of this method is that nutrients are transported upwards, along with the water, so that they are no longer available to the finer roots at the bottom of the pot but tend to accumulate on the surface of the soil which becomes crusty and full of salts.
Watering from the top (see illustration 1b) is recommended for most houseplants. Always pour the water directly on to the soil, not on to the plant. The soil will become well moistened and nutrients contained in the water will be distributed evenly from the top downwards so that the finest roots are able to absorb them.
Epiphytic bromeliads should be watered by tipping the water ***straight into their funnels*** (see illustration 2a) as they have special cells at the funnel base for absorbing water.
Submerging (see illustration 2b) is the best method for epiphytes and orchids as this allows the water-permeable compost to absorb the moisture properly. Submerging is also ideal for plants in hanging baskets or ferns in lattice baskets. It is also a good first aid measure for plants whose rootstocks have completely dried out.

The ten golden rules of watering

1. Always consider any special ***requirements that different species may have.*** Find out whether each particular species needs lots of water or very little.
2. ***During their growth phase*** and at flowering time (usually in spring and summer) water plentifully and often.
3. ***During their rest phase*** (in autumn and particularly in winter), reduce the amounts of water gradually and later water only as much as is needed to prevent the rootstock from drying out.
4. You will need to ***water more often if plants are in:***
   - dry, warm rooms;
   - bright, sunny positions;
   - clay pots;
   - small pots that have become filled with matted roots so that the plants have hardly any compost left to store water.
5. ***Water plants less often:***
   - in cool rooms with high humidity;
   - in positions with little light;
   - in plastic pots;
   - in pots with sufficient compost around the roots as the compost will be able to hold moisture.
6. ***Use only lukewarm water.*** Cold water makes it more difficult for the plant to absorb nutrients, hinders growth and can lead to root decay.
7. ***Never pour water on the leaves and flowers*** as this may cause spots on the leaves and fungal infections.

8. ***Never water plants in full sunlight.*** Drops of water can act like magnifying glasses and cause burns on the leaves.
9. ***Do not water plants in the same place every time*** because this will create little channels in the potting compost, through which the water will run straight down without allowing the rootstock to soak up moisture.
10. ***Be careful with saucers or pot holders*** underneath the plant pot as it is often impossible to see if surplus water has accumulated in them. Waterlogging drives air out of the compost and then the roots will be unable to absorb water or nutrients. The result is root decay, which will eventually lead to the death of the entire plant. In principle, check the saucer or pot holder about half an hour after watering.

3. Moisture meters are useful watering aids for beginners.

4. Automatic watering systems

a) Insert clay pegs into the soil and place their water pipes in a container filled with water.

b) Absorbent fabric is able to supply water to several plants (in clay pots) at the same. A tilted draining board is excellent.

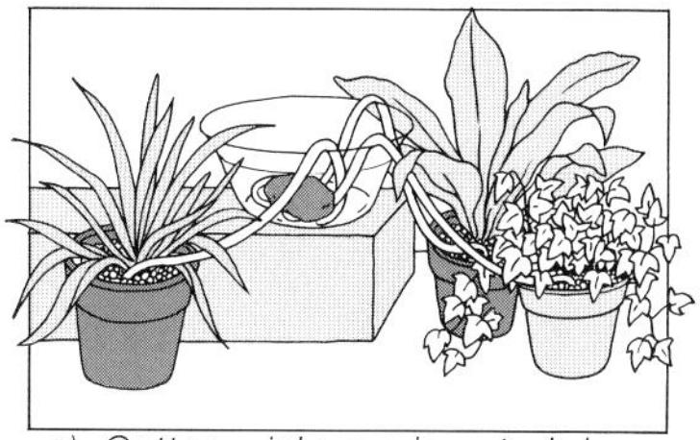

c) Cotton wicks are inserted deep in the soil; the other end is weighted down with a stone in a bucket of water.

Automatic watering

A range of devices is obtainable in the gardening trade for use by those people who are unable to water regularly or might have to be away from home for long periods of time. Ask for advice about these at your garden centre, however, as some systems are only suitable for short-term, weekend use, while others will supply water to your plants over a period of several weeks. Some good methods are described below.

Clay pegs (see illustration 4a) are filled with water and inserted in the compost. Moisture is supplied at a constant rate through the clay. As the moisture is released, it is also replenished through a pipe leading from a storage container. A 10–litre ($17^1/_2$ pt) bucket can supply a plant with water for up to a month.

Absorbent fabrics (see illustration 4b) can supply water to several plants at once. Fill a sink to serve as a reservoir. The mat should reach from the sink to the draining board but should not hang over the edge of the draining board as this will cause water to drip on to the floor. Plants in clay pots will soak up water from the drenched fabric, which means that they can regulate their own water supply.

Water-absorbent wicks (see illustration 4c), made, for example, of cotton or fibreglass, can be pushed deep into the compost or threaded on a large darning needle and pulled up from below and out through the top. The other end of the wick should be placed in a bucket of water and weighted down with a stone so that it cannot slip out.

NB: The water level in the bucket must be higher than the plant pots so that the system will function properly. The wicks should not be allowed to hang down in loops or the water will drip off them before ever reaching the flowerpot.

Watering

Such a window position can become a death trap for ferns on account of hot, dry, centrally heated air during the winter.

Humidity

Country of origin: Many houseplants originate from tropical regions and are accustomed to naturally high humidity, particularly:

- plants from tropical rain forests, which live in an atmosphere of steaming heat and a humidity of up to 90% all year round;
- plants from tropical mountain forests, which have adapted to intensely bright light, cool temperatures, mists and very high humidity.

Plants from more arid regions, for example, cacti and succulents from desert regions, or subtropical plants from dry areas, which are often equipped with water storage organs and other measures to protect themselves against water loss through evaporation, can be kept as houseplants, even at low humidity.

Moisture: Nearly all plants are able to maintain the right balance in their water supply by absorbing water and then allowing it to evaporate (see p. 7). This happens by means of tiny pores which open mainly in the daytime in order to absorb carbon dioxide from the air. During this process, they also release oxygen and moisture from their cells.

Too much moisture: If the air is completely saturated with moisture (a state of affairs that rarely occurs in their natural environment), the plant can no longer release water through evaporation and the result is that water and nutrients are no longer absorbed. The consequences are:

- a temporary cessation of growth;
- the plants become susceptible to attack by fungal diseases.

Too little moisture: Dry air and high temperatures speed up evaporation. Even with frequent watering, the roots can no longer balance the loss of water in the leaves quickly enough and the following happens:

- the leaf tips turn brown;
- the leaves dry out;
- the flowers and buds drop off.

When plants drip: Do not be surprised if philodendrons, *Dieffenbachia* or other houseplants produce tiny droplets even though you have not watered or sprayed them. This is not a symptom of disease but a simple reaction in the plant which has been unable to evaporate as much as it needs to in the position it has been given and needs to get rid of some water. It will secrete more moisture, thus enabling its roots to absorb larger amounts of water.

What is relative humidity?

One of the most important factors of proper plant care is "relative humidity", which indicates, as a percentage, how much water the air contains compared to complete saturation (100%) at equal temperatures.

Humidity can be measured quite easily with a hygrometer, obtainable from specialist gardening suppliers.

Values for plant care:

- below 50% = low humidity;
- 50–60% = medium humidity;
- above 60% = high humidity.

The prevailing humidity levels are around 60–90% in the tropical countries of origin of many houseplants, so you should maintain at least a medium level of humidity in a room where plants are kept (see pp. 34–5).

The correct amount of humidity

More humidity is required by:

- plants with large, soft leaves, such as *Sparrmannia* and *Ensete*;
- plants with delicate, thin leaves, such as *Caladium* and maidenhair fern (*Adiantum*);
- epiphytic plants, such as many orchids, bromeliads and *Tillandsia*;
- ferns.

Less humidity is required by:

- plants with leathery, tough leaves such as the rubber tree (*Ficus*) and *Monstera deliciosa*;
- plants with reduced leaves or needles, such as *Cupressus macrocarpa*;
- cacti;
- succulents, such as *Aeonium*.

Humidity and warmth: The higher the temperature, the more water vapour the air can absorb. If the amount of water remains the same and the temperature rises, the air actually becomes drier. When this happens, the plants lose more water through evaporation so that they then require twice as much moisture.

Winter

By far the most difficult time for houseplants is winter. This is when they usually have to cope with a position on a windowsill above a radiator and various other unpleasant conditions. Many die, for one of several possible reasons.

The air in a room is particularly dry in winter (often humidity levels are at 15–40%). The minimum acceptable level of humidity for most flowering and foliage plants is about 50%.

During the winter, the air is particularly cool and dry. This means that when you air the room, dry air streams in and robs the existing air of further moisture.

NB: During the winter, the climate in the room needs to be enriched with moisture to ensure the well-being of the plants.

Raising humidity

The humidity surrounding a houseplant can be increased in any of several simple ways.

Humidity through spraying

Using a misting bottle will not raise the humidity in the entire room but it can still be useful.
Indirect spraying (see illustration 2a) creates a short-term supply of moisture all around the plant. This is recommended for plants with hairy leaves that cannot stand direct misting and for others whose leaves and flowers tend to become spotty or whose buds might begin to rot.
Never spray directly on to: begonias, *Calceolaria* hybrids, *Codiaeum*, *Dieffenbachia*, *Fatsia*, x *Fatshedera lizei*, *Hippeastrum* hybrids, mimosa, *Peperomia*, African violets (*Saintpaulia ionantha* hybrids), gloxinias (*Sinningia* hybrids) or *Streptocarpus.*
Direct spraying (see illustration 2b) provides direct moisture and imitates the natural formation of dew drops, which is required by *Tillandsia* and other epiphytes such as *Platycerium.*
NB: Use soft water, adjust the misting bottle to a fine setting, do not spray the flowers and preferably spray in the mornings and not in direct sunlight.

1. A bottle garden with its own mini-climate
An ideal home for plants in dry indoor air. Insert a drainage layer of Hortag and use small plants.

Trays on the windowsill

The worst plight is experienced by houseplants that are placed on windowsills during the winter months and are constantly plagued by hot air rising up from the radiators beneath. Some very simple measures can be taken to improve the living conditions of such plants.
Use an evaporator tray (see illustration 3): Large dishes with a grid insert are available in the gardening trade. They are placed on the windowsill, filled with water and the grid is inserted. The plants do not come into direct contact with the water but are surrounded by evaporating moisture.

- Advantage: You can accommodate several plants in such a tray.
- Alternative: The same result can be achieved by using any large, flat dishes filled first with Hortag, pebbles or gravel and then with water. Arrange the plants so that they do not suffer from "wet feet".

Make narrow windowsills wider: for example, by laying wooden boards on the windowsills. The hot, dry air rising up from the radiators is deflected by this device and will no longer flow past the leaves of the plants on the sill.

2. Create humid air through spraying
a) Spraying above the plant will supply indirect humidity.
b) Tillandsia and other epiphytes should be sprayed directly.

Install a wide plant basin: This method is usually the most successful. A plant basin of whatever dimensions you choose can be used like a windowbox.

- Make sure that you choose a plant basin that is wide enough to cover the entire area of the windowsill and radiator.
- Stand plastic bowls or dishes inside the basin or line the basin with foil or something similar to make it watertight. Then insert a layer of Hortag or pebbles, pour in water and stand the plants on the pebbles.
- Alternatively, you can insert a layer of Hortag or peat in the basin and then bed the plants in this up to the tops of the pots.

NB: These plants should be planted in closed pots (without a drainage hole) so that they are not permanently exposed to moisture from below.

My tip: Evaporator dishes need constant attention and the regular addition of water. Clean them out once a week as lime, bacteria and algae tend to become deposited in them.

Moisture for individual pots

● Place Hortag, clay granules or fine bark mulch between individual plant pots and pot holders (see illustration 4a) and keep this moist.

● Stand individual pots on a small, upturned dish or balance them on four, halved corks in a larger dish filled with water (see illustration 4b). The moisture will evaporate upwards, flowing past the plant itself.

My tip: The smaller the evaporation tray, the more often it will need filling with water.

Electric humidifiers

These devices raise the humidity all around the plant and guarantee that humidity levels are raised in the entire room. Humidifiers work on various principles:

Misters, which cause water to be sprayed in the finest drops through centrifugal force.

Evaporators heat the water until it turns to water vapour.

Condensing devices blow or suck air through a moist filter. They are very cheap to run but require a regular filter change.

Further tips for raising humidity

If you do not wish to keep an electric humidifier running constantly, you can employ several methods at once in a room, as most of the methods described below will only raise the humidity in the immediate vicinity of the plant.

Mechanical humidifiers: Hang these on your radiator in winter and refill them with water every day.

Evaporator dishes serve the same purpose for open fireplaces, boilers, etc.

Aquariums, which have a constant movement of water due to a filter pump, will also make a small contribution towards raising the humidity in a room.

Spring stones set amid plants are gaining in popularity as they are extremely attractive and create a pleasant atmosphere in a room.

In summer, fresh outdoor air is ideal for stabilizing houseplants during the warm season of the year. Particularly during, and immediately after, a rain shower the air will be laden with moisture. At such times, stand your houseplants at an open window or on a balcony or patio.

3. Trays for the windowsill
This is ideal for providing several plants with humid air. Lay a grid in the tray and pour in water to just below the grid.

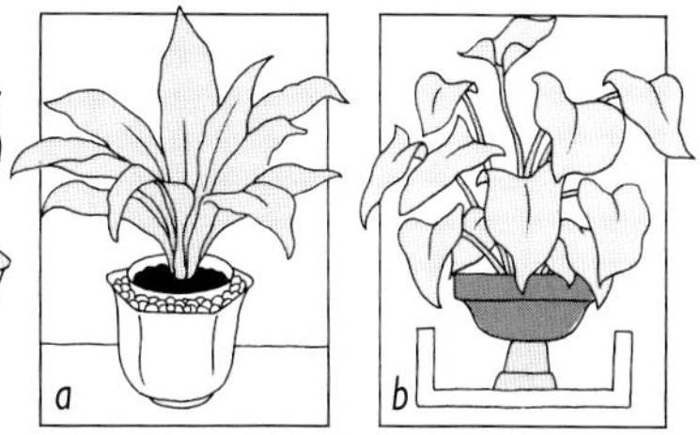

4. Humidity for individual plant pots
a) Bed the plant pot in a larger pot filled with Hortag, peat or clay granules.
b) Stand the plant on an upside-down pot in a large dish filled with water.

A large number of plants, or several large plants, have more soil and roots and can therefore store much more moisture than a few plants in small pots. If you have several plants, or large ones, it is worth grouping them together. The water that is evaporated will benefit them all in the form of humidity.

Moisture-producing places, such as bathrooms and kitchens, are more suitable for moisture-loving plants than offices with a very dry atmosphere. At the same time, you have to remember that such places are aired frequently and longer. Protect plants in an office from cold air and draughts.

The delicate maidenhair fern (top left) requires different fertilizing to the robust Gerbera or Tillandsia (a bromeliad) (see p. 37, left). A wide range of nutrients, in various forms, is available from garden centres etc.

Fertilizing

Although plants are the only living things that are able to utilize sunlight directly for their own growth, they are still unable to live on light and air alone. Houseplants will not thrive without the right amounts of plant nutrients.

Plant nutrients

A well-balanced supply of nutrients will ensure that plants thrive and produce flowers. At the same time, nutrients will help to make the plants resistant to pests and diseases. Most plants absorb nutrients, together with water, through their fine roots but even the leaves are able to absorb small quantities of nutrients. The most unusual plants in this respect are bromeliads, *Tillandsia* or orchids, which live and grow on trees and have specially adapted devices inside their funnel-shaped leaf shafts to absorb water and nutrients. Water should be delivered directly into their funnels (see illustration 2a, p. 30) and they should be fertilized in the same way.

Every plant will require fairly large amounts of the ***main nutrients*** (see table, p. 39). Among these are nitrogen (N), phosphorus (P), potassium (K), calcium (Ca), magnesium (Mg) and sulphur (S).

The trace elements (micro-nutrients) are necessary for the healthy growth of the plant and are just as important as the main nutrients but are absorbed in much smaller quantities. Among these are iron (Fe), copper (Cu), manganese (Mn), molybdenum (Mo), zinc (Zn), chlorine (Cl) and boron (B).

Nutrient balance: Houseplants must be fertilized as essential nutrients are generally only present in restricted amounts in potting compost and are used up fairly quickly. The most important thing to remember is that nutrients have to be combined in the proper proportions when fertilizing houseplants. Over- or under-dosing with a particular nutrient may leave the plant unable to absorb other nutrients, even if they are present in a plentiful supply. For example, if there is too much or too little calcium in the water or compost, the plants will be unable to absorb other nutrients.

Compound fertilizer

Good compound fertilizers contain the main nutrients and many trace elements in proportions that are plant-friendly and well balanced.

● Compound fertilizer can be obtained in almost any form, liquid, pulverized or solid, as granules, in tablet form, or as small sticks or cones.

● It may contain organic components or synthetic substances ("artificial" fertilizer).

● It comes in various grades, containing varying amounts of certain elements, so that nitrogen, phosphorus or potassium is emphasized, depending on the requirements of the plant. This is very important because each of these elements is responsible in different ways for supporting the growth and well-being of the plant (see table, right).

● You can also obtain fertilizers in different concentrations: concentrated, high-percentage fertilizers, and light, low-percentage ones.

● Depending on their effect, a distinction is made between fast-working, compound fertilizers and controlled-release fertilizers.

Be sure to read what is written on the packaging. Compound fertilizers are easier to handle if you know exactly what they contain. Many manufacturers indicate the proportions of the main nutrients in percentages on the packaging. The sequence is always the same – N (nitrogen), P (phosphorus), K (potassium) – and is usually indicated in figures, for example:

● 8/6/12 (or 8:6:12) which means that this fertilizer consists of 8% nitrogen, 6% phosphorus (to be more exact, P_2O_2 = water-soluble phosphate) and 12% potassium (actually K_2O) = water-soluble potassium oxide) and is, therefore, a compound fertilizer with an emphasis on potassium.

● 7/3/6 indicates a light fertilizer with an emphasis on nitrogen, containing 7% nitrogen, 3% phosphorus and 6% potassium.

Buying tip: The prices of compound fertilizers vary considerably due to the varying concentrations of nutrients. You will have to use more of the light fertilizers than the concentrated ones in order to obtain the same fertilizing results. They are usually cheaper but are also used up more quickly.

The main nutrients and their effect

Nutrients	The right dose	Overdosing	Lack of nutrients	First aid for symptoms of nutrient deficiency
nitrogen (N)	encourages the growth of leaves, shoots and roots	lanky growth, spongy tissue, susceptibility to aphids and fungi	older leaves turn yellowish, deformed growth	hornmeal, dried blood, compound fertilizers with an emphasis on nitrogen
phos-phorus (P)	encourages the formation of flowers and ripe seed	metabolic disturbances, lack of iron, impaired formation of roots	red brown discoloration of leaves, leaves grow sharply upright, weak flowering, hardly any seed	bonemeal, guano, liquid superphosphate, compound fertilizers with an emphasis on phosphorus
potassium (K)	encourages firm tissue and the formation of roots	impedes growth, lack of magnesium and calcium	older leaves become discoloured and brownish around the edges, then die	potassium compound, guano, wood ash, com-pound fertilizers with potassium emphasis
magnesium (Mg)	encourages the formation of chlorophyll and firm tissue	encourages susceptibility to infestation with aphids and spider mites, poss-ibly lack of potassium	older leaves turn yellow, the veins remain green	magnesium lime, algae lime, wood ash
calcium (Ca)	encourages growth of roots and regulates the growth of shoots	leads to lack of phos-phorus and reduced growth of roots	buds die off	calcium carbonate, algae lime, guano
sulphur (S)	encourages metabolic processes	results in dwarfism	the youngest leaves turn yellow; rare	instead of fertilizing, change the compost

Organic fertilizers
More and more manufacturers are producing houseplant fertilizers based on natural (animal or vegetable) substances. Organic fertilizing is ideal for establishing a harmonious, long-term programme of plant care. If, however, an acute lack of nutrients is diagnosed, you should use a synthetic "artificial" fertilizer, as the nutrients bound in such salts are immediately available for absorption by the plant.
In ***mineral fertilizers***, the nutrients are bound to synthetic salts which dissolve easily and can be used at once by the plant. A lack of nutrients is thus easily remedied, but the danger of overfertilizing is then also greater as the plants have no other option but to absorb these "instant meals". Too much nitrogen, for example, will cause the cells to swell and become spongy. This will make the plant susceptible to diseases and pests.
Another problem is that the compost in the plant pot may become saturated with salts. The micro-organisms in the compost will then find it increasingly difficult to survive and your plants will suffer accordingly, because the micro-organisms are no longer fulfilling their function. A healthy environment in a plant pot really is a matter of the delicate balance of so many important factors.
The plant is now able to obtain nutrients only from the artificial fertilizer, on which it becomes increasingly dependent. If mistakes are made in fertilizing, weakened plants quickly will succumb to diseases or pests.

The correct fertilizer

Green plant fertilizer should be used for foliage plants. These compound fertilizers, which have an emphasis on nitrogen, can be obtained in liquid form or as tablets, small sticks or cones. Liquid fertilizer is immediately effective; the solid forms are usually controlled-release fertilizers with an effective range of four to six weeks.
Flowering fertilizer should be used for flowering plants. The proportion of nitrogen is less in these fertilizers but phosphorus and potassium are present in larger proportions.
Orchid fertilizer should be used for orchids and bromeliads as well as for other plants that react sensitively to mineral salts. These fertilizers contain far fewer mineral salts and can be mixed with water for watering or sprayed on the leaves.
Cactus fertilizer should be used for cacti from dry desert regions, as well as for succulents. It is poor in nitrogen and calcium but is quite rich in phosphorus and potassium.
Ericaceous (rhododendron) fertilizer or fertilizer for marsh plants should be used for azaleas, heathers and hortensia hydrangeas, which all require an acid soil and fertilizers that are low in mineral salts.
Leaf fertilizers should be well diluted and sprayed on to the leaves. They are particularly recommended as a remedy for damaged roots. Many preparations that can be sprayed on also contain vitamins and trace elements, which will encourage growth. Indoor gardeners are advised to employ leaf fertilizing as a special treatment in addition to regular fertilizing. It is particularly recommended for balancing the lack of a single nutrient. If a deficiency of iron is diagnosed, iron preparations will provide fast relief.
NB: This fertilizer is not suitable for very hairy leaves.
Special fertilizers should be used for plants grown in hydroculture or special granules (see p. 42).

My tip: Make sure you read the manufacturer's instructions for dosing with mineral fertilizers and find out about the individual needs of the plants (whether they require large or small amounts of nutrients, see right) so that they are not overfed. It is better to fertilize too little than too much.

Organic fertilizers provide plants with a "wholefood" menu consisting of animal or vegetable products. First, however, these have to be broken down by organisms in the soil and converted into nutrients that are accessible to the plant, which means they take much longer to be effective. The restricted space in the flowerpot means that soil organisms often do not flourish well, indeed, many commercial composts have a very low count of soil organisms. However, some very effective organic fertilizers are now on sale, intended for pot plants and enriched with additional micro-organisms. These powdered fertilizers are mixed with the potting compost when the plants are potted, then regularly sprinkled on the compost and mixed in with a small stick. Always water thoroughly.
The danger of overfertilizing and creating an accumulation of salts is hardly possible with this kind of fertilizing, and repotting is required less often.
Organic-mineral fertilizers endeavour to combine the advantages of both processes. These are fast-working, mineral fertilizers for houseplants, which are mixed with organic components such as humic acid or guano.

Fertilize according to the requirements of the plants

In order to feed your houseplants properly and according to their individual needs, you will need some knowledge of the requirements of the different species. Just like humans, plants have different likes and dislikes.
"Big eaters" are plants that use up their nutrient supply very quickly and must be fertilized weekly during their main growth phase. Among these are:

- foliage plants that produce masses of leaves in a very short time, such as *Caladium* or *Sparrmannia*;
- flowering plants that are expected to produce masses of flowers, such as *Gloriosa superba* 'Rothschildiana', hibiscus (*Hibiscus rosa-sinensis*) or passion flower (*Passiflora*).

Desert cacti will only display their enchanting flowers after overwintering in a bright, cool position. Special cactus fertilizer is recommended.

"Small eaters" often require nutrients in fairly low doses and no more frequently than every three to four weeks. When using solid compound fertilizers, give the plants only half of the recommended dose or, if it is liquid fertilizer, use double the amount of water. Among these types are:

- foliage plants that produce few or small leaves, such as *Beaucarnea recurvata*, *Ceropegia linearis* subsp. *woodii*, *Cupressus macrocarpa*, *Fittonia albivenis* Verschaffeltii Group, *Peperomia*, *Sansevieria*, *Senecio rowleyanus* and *Yucca*;
- cacti (with the exception of leaf cacti);
- succulents;
- orchids;
- ferns;
- many species of palm.

Nutrition specialists (see table, p. 40): The gardening trade has introduced commercial compound fertilizers for cacti, succulents, orchids, bromeliads and azaleas, which are exactly suited to the requirements of these particular plants.

Plants in special mediums, such as Hortag or other granules, should be fed only with fertilizers that have been specially designed for them (see how to fertilize in hydroculture, p. 42).

The ten golden rules of fertilizing

1. Only fertilize plants during their growth phase. For most plants this means that you should begin fertilizing cautiously at the beginning to middle of the first month of spring. As daylight increases, the new shoots will begin to grow. Gradually increase the supply of nutrients and then, from early autumn onwards, reduce it again.

2. Plants that flower throughout the winter (such as cyclamen or camellias) have different growth cycles and should be fertilized in different ways before and after flowering (see Flowering plants and their care, p. 10, and Foliage plants and their care, p. 14).

3. Plants with definite rest phases (such as passion flower, *Passiflora*), during which the plant should hardly be watered at all and should be kept in a dark, cool position, should not be fertilized either. Plants with a medium rest phase (such as *Spathiphyllum*), which are grown in a bright, warm position, should be fertilized every four weeks during winter but in very sparing doses.

4. Never fertilize a dry rootstock as the nutrient salts may burn the fine roots. Always water the plant before fertilizing.

5. Freshly repotted plants should not be fertilized for at least six weeks. The nutrients in the new compost should last until then.

6. Do not fertilize sick plants.

7. Do not fertilize young, small plants with few roots and later do so sparingly every four weeks.

8. The amount of fertilizer will depend on the nutrient requirements of the plant and on its size. Large plants need more food than small ones.

9. If in doubt, fertilize often in small amounts rather than seldom in large doses.

10. When using mineral compound fertilizers, read the instructions on the packaging carefully. Use only half of the recommended dose or use a special fertilizer for cacti, succulents, orchids, palms, ferns and bromeliads (see p. 40).

Overfertilized plants

Depending on the main nutrient in the fertilizer, various symptoms may appear if too much is given (see table, p. 39). The danger of overfertilizing is much greater with mineral compound fertilizers. There are a few symptoms to watch out for.

- If white salt deposits and crusts appear on the outside of clay pots or on the surface of the compost.
- If the leaves of the plants wilt or become deformed and you feel sure you have not made mistakes in watering and there is no indication of pests.
- If the leaves produce brown spots and blackish-brown burns along their edges.

Prevention: Plants that are several years old and can cope with repotting should be planted in fresh compost every year.

First aid: If you are sure your houseplants have received too much fertilizer and are already showing symptoms of damage, you can save them by taking the plant out of the pot and submerging the rootstock in water for about fifteen minutes. This will dissolve and wash out the surplus salts. Soak the pot too and scrub off any salt deposits with a brush. Then allow the rootstock to drip dry and replant the plant in the clean pot with fresh compost.

How to fertilize in hydroculture

A supply of nutrients is particularly important when using this form of culture as the plant is exclusively fed by the fertilizer provided and does not receive any other nutrients from soil or compost. Two types of fertilizer have proved to be successful.

Nutrient solutions, which can be mixed with water. Read the instructions for dosage on the packaging very carefully.

Fertilizer batteries containing ion exchangers can be fastened beneath the inner culture pot. They are particularly useful because they remove calcium, chlorine and other harmful substances from the water over a period of four to six months.

The advantages are:
- you will not need to fertilize for long periods of time;
- overfertilizing is impossible with this method;
- you can use mains water for watering – in fact this is necessary as the salts dissolved in it are required for the working of the ion exchange process.

My tip: This is the ideal way to supply nutrients to houseplants in an office and to foliage plants owned by people who are out at work all day.

Replenishing nutrients
- If you use a nutrient solution, you will have to renew the entire amount after about six to eight weeks and also rinse the plant well.
- If you use fertilizer batteries, you should renew the water at the same time as you change the batteries, which is every four to six months; also rinse the plant well.
- For plants in hydroculture, leave the plants in their container but remove this from the pot holder. Spray slightly warm water over the Hortag and the pot for about five to ten minutes so that everything is well rinsed off. While waiting, clean the pot holder thoroughly.
Allow the plant to drip dry, insert the water level indicator, put everything back into the pot holder and fill the main vessel with fresh water containing a nutrient solution or a new fertilizer battery.

How to apply fertilizer correctly

Type of fertilizer	Use	Effect
liquid fertilizer	mix with water	fast
powder, crystals	dissolve in water	fast
foaming tablets	dissolve in water	fast
sticks, cones	push into the compost	controlled-release fertilizer: the nutrients are released over a period of 4–6 months
slowly dissolving granules	mix with the compost when planting	controlled-release fertilizer: the nutrients are released over a period of 4–6 months
leaf sprays	spray on leaves (not on hairy leaves)	fast

Alternative plant fortifiers
These substances, which are derived from plants, are not considered to be primary sources of nutrients but are rich in trace elements, vitamins, hormones, enzymes and other substances which encourage growth. They help to strengthen the plant and encourage its development and resistance to disease.
Marine algae extract is derived from brown algae and sprayed on to the leaves in a very diluted form, just like leaf fertilizer. Use this substance if your plant is weakened due to lack of proper care or disease. It will fortify the plant's resistance on a broad basis.
When diluted, ***mare's tail extract*** can be sprayed on the leaves or given in water when watering the plant in the normal way. Treatment with this solution will strengthen the cells of the plant and act as a prevention against fungal disease.
Valerian extract can also be used for watering or spraying. It promotes the well-being of soil organisms and encourages better flower formation.
Camomile tea: Add 1 litre (1³¹⁄₄₄ pt) boiling water to 10 g dried camomile flowers. Allow this to cool and strain it. Dilute as 3 parts water to 1 part tea and use to water the plant. This will encourage growth and resistance to disease.

If things are not going well inside the plant pot, the plant will not be able to grow properly.

Repotting

Even in a pot, roots never stop growing in their constant search for new sources of nutrients. The compost soon gets used up and the pot becomes too tight. Repotting is necessary for the healthy development of your houseplants.

All about soil and compost

People often ask why it is not sufficient for the roots to have enough soil to sit in and to be nourished with fertilizer. In actual fact, plants can be cared for in this manner in hydroculture, while growing plants in granules (see p. 54) also works well. Even then, however, you still have to change the water or pot every so often.

Repotting so that the plant can grow: In the wild, whether it is a dwarf moss or a tree, every plant maintains a state of balance in respect of growth. This means that the root system has grown to exactly the point where it can best supply the above-ground parts with nutrients and water. There is a balance between what goes on above ground and below ground. With plants that are grown in pots, the roots are unable to develop freely as they would in the wild, in accordance with their genetic programming. Not enough space or not enough soil containing nutrients will both hamper the growth of roots. Fewer roots means that less plant material can be supplied with what it requires to grow and so the growth of the above-soil parts of plants in containers is much slower.

Repotting rule 1: If you want your plants to grow larger and bushier, you should repot them once a year and give them a larger pot with fresh compost each time (see p. 50).

When to repot

A glance at your plant, the soil and the pot will give you some idea.

1. When the young leaves of new shoots remain small.
2. If the plant does not seem to grow properly or fails to flower.
3. If, when removed from the pot, the rootstock appears to have used up all the soil and the roots are densely matted.
4. If the roots are growing out of the drainage hole in the pot.
5. If root tips are peeking out of the soil at the top of the pot.
6. If the roots look ill – are blackish, spongy or smell bad – or have died.
7. If the roots look matted or are growing in a circle at the bottom of the pot because they are searching for more space.
8. If white sediment is forming on clay pots.
9. If clay pots are covered in green algae or if moss is growing on the compost. Both are indicators of overwatering, waterlogging or of compost that has become hard and dense.
10. If the plant has been standing in surplus water for a long time.

My tip: The ideal time for repotting is always at the beginning of the new growth phase. For most plants, this is the first month of spring. This moment will be signalled by the formation of new shoots. Never repot a plant during flowering time or during its rest phase.

Repotting rule 2: If the plant has reached the point where you do not wish it to grow any larger, repot it only every two to three years. Renew the soil but keep the same size of pot.

My tip: Some plants are reliable bloomers even if their root space is restricted, for example, *Clivia miniata* and *Hippeastrum* hybrids.

Repotting to provide a renewed supply of nutrients: Plants do not just absorb water and nutrients through their roots; they also secrete metabolic waste matter, an accumulation of which can impede growth. In the wild, these substances are partially recycled by micro-organisms in the soil. In a flowerpot, this process can only function in a very limited way and, over time, the waste matter accumulates in the confined space of the pot.
Furthermore, it is not only plant-friendly substances that are introduced to the pot when watering. Substances that are harmful to plants, or salts that bind mineral nutrients, will gradually become deposited in the potting medium. This encourages the soil to become richer in lime and salts so that the plant is no longer able to absorb nutrients properly and becomes weakened in growth and resistance.

Repotting rule 3: Growing a plant in a pot eventually causes the compost to be used up. This has to be renewed at least every two to three years.

Soil

Plants grow and thrive in the wild where they are part of the natural cycle of birth and death. Just as they derive nutrients and water from the soil, they also return their waste products to it and are later converted into nutrient bases for new life when they die.
These regular cycles are interrupted in the case of houseplants as the plants derive nutrients and water from the soil in a one-sided process. The indoor gardener is the one who has to make sure the supply continues.

Garden soil: Never use pure garden soil for your houseplants. The quality of such soil varies and, for this reason, it may be too light or too heavy for growing plants in pots, or may contain too many or too few nutrients. Garden soil also often contains the seeds of weeds or germs that cause disease. If used at all, garden soil should be only one component of a soil mixture.

My tip: Garden soil should always be used after it has been sieved and sterilized in your oven at a temperature of 200 °C (400 °F) for 30 minutes.

Garden compost should likewise be only one component of a soil mixture as pure compost contains too many nutrients. Garden compost should also be sieved before being used in a potting compost mixture (see table). Never use semi-mature compost. It must be completely mature and free of fermenting substances.

The right soil/compost

Plant groups	Recommended ready-made potting composts	Recipes for your own mixtures
Most houseplants, also: ● leaf cacti ● ferns ● bromeliads ● palms ● camellias	● standard potting compost ● bark compost ● peat-free and other potting composts containing little peat (see p. 52)	2 parts garden soil; 1 part ripe compost, leaf mould compost or bark compost; 1 part fine Hortag or pumice sand; a little hornmeal and crushed lava meal
cacti, succulents	cactus compost	3 parts pumice grit; 1 part quartz sand or lava grit; 1 part ripe compost, leaf mould compost or bark compost
azaleas, hortensia hydrangeas, camellias, heathers	ericaceous (rhododendron) compost	1 part ripe compost, leaf mould or bark compost; 1 part garden soil; 2 parts hygromulch or wood fibre
orchids as well as epiphytic bromeliads and ferns	orchid composts	1 part crumbled cork; 1 part pine bark; 1 part polystyrene flakes; ½ part ripe compost; ½ part charcoal; 2 g calcium carbonate per litre of mixture
palms palm ferns	palm composts or standard potting compost	1 part ripe compost; 1 part hygromulch or wood fibre; 1 part sand; ½ part polystyrene flakes; ½ part loam

Hortag is the ideal, easy-care compost for plants in an office as they only need watering and fertilizing at long intervals.

Potting compost

Basically, this is any medium used for growing plants in pots. Potting compost is always a mixture of different substances and may even contain no proper soil at all. It can be mixed at home or bought ready-mixed and packed.

NB: There is a large range of ready-made mixtures of varying quality and at very different prices. Do not be stingy. Choose only high-quality ready-made compost for your houseplants to give them a good start and help them to flourish. Potting compost endeavours to provide the plants with the best possible medium for growing and flourishing in the unnatural conditions of an indoor environment. It has to have very special qualities.

The ideal compost should be:

- ***Loose and permeable*** so that the roots can breathe and develop properly and so that there is no waterlogging, which would drive the oxygen out of the compost. This would cause the roots to decay and the plant's growth would suffer.
- Able to ***store water,*** so that the compost does not dry out too fast, as water is needed to help the plant to absorb nutrients and also to transport them.

- ***Structurally stable***, which means that it does not rot down too fast, remains loose for a long time and does not become dense. It should also provide a firm footing for the roots. Fast-rotting substances have the disadvantage that they release additional nutrients during this process. On the other hand, structurally stable composts guarantee an even distribution and release of nutrients.
- Able to ***store nutrients***, which means that the nutrients remain bound in the compost so that they are at the disposal of the plant when it needs them. Sand, for example, cannot hold nutrients they are washed away with the water.
- ***Free of diseases and weeds*** so that the plant will remain healthy and without any competition.
- ***Slightly acid*** – 5–6.5 in the pH range. The acidity factor (see p. 28) is one of the most important properties of the compost and the action of micro-organisms in the compost is directly dependent on this, as is how well the plants will be able to absorb nutrients. The pH value of the compost also determines how well the plants will grow.

The most important components of good compost

- Peat or peat substitutes are able to bind water and air, are poor in nutrients and structurally stable. They keep compost loose for longer.
- Loam stores nutrients and water particularly well and releases it in favourable doses to the plants. Further, its mineral components are released very slowly, so it is structurally stable.
- Sand makes compost water-permeable and prevents waterlogging.
- Polystyrene flakes and similar materials prevent waterlogging and keep the compost mixture porous.
- Hortag and other clay granules are structurally stable and poor in nutrients. They are able to store water and air very well and to release them on demand.

Suitable compost

If you wish, you can mix your own potting compost (see table, p. 47). The effort is definitely worthwhile for garden owners who usually have a supply of garden soil or garden compost anyway. The majority of houseplants will manage very well in standard potting composts but there is a small group with some special requirements.

Standard compost: is suitable for most flowering and foliage houseplants. It is universally usable and consists of 60–80% sedge peat and 40–20% clay or loam, including fast-working and controlled-release fertilizers and trace elements.

Flower compost: is a term that is used to refer to a range of composts of varying degrees of quality.

Peat-based composts: consist mainly of sedge peat with added lime and nutrients. They can be used for very leafy plants but should be used with restraint in order to curb the exploitation of natural wetlands and peat bogs.

Special composts for cacti and succulents: are water-permeable as well as poor in nitrogen and organic matter. NB: Leaf cacti should be grown in ordinary flower potting composts.

Ericaceous (rhododendron) composts: possess a very low pH factor of 4.5–5.5 and contain large amounts of peat.

Orchid composts: should be poor in nutrients and air- and water-permeable. They comprise coarse peat fibre, bark, polystyrene flakes, charcoal and mineral substances such as pumice gravel, lava or Perlite. Their pH factor is usually around 5–6.

Epiphyte planting medium: is made out of chopped marsh moss, *Osmunda* fern roots and coarse peat fibre. You can also use orchid composts for epiphytes.

Clay granules: are tiny clay beads of various sizes, which can store water, allow air to penetrate and are structurally stable. Their main task is to provide a firm hold for the roots of the plants.

Hortag pellets: are specially made for hydroculture (see p. 54).

My tip: When repotting houseplants, do not use seeding compost or compost for pricking out young plants. Neither of these composts contains any fertilizer, or hardly any, and therefore they are only suitable for sowing or propagation.

How to repot

Always bear in mind the following rules when you repot a plant.

The ten golden rules of repotting

1. Never repot plants during flowering time or their rest phase.
2. Never repot plants with a completely dried-out rootstock; always give them some water beforehand.
3. Damaged or sick (blackish or spongy) roots should be cut off.
4. Carefully remove old soil or compost from the surface, sides and below the rootstock.
5. Do not damage the very finest roots.
6. Fine roots that have formed a densely matted mass can be cut off or trimmed.
7. Any injured fleshy roots should be dusted with charcoal powder so that no disease-inducing germs can penetrate the plant.
8. Use only thoroughly cleaned containers (soak clay pots in water for one or two hours).
9. After repotting, water the plant thoroughly.
10. Do not fertilize a plant that has been repotted for at least six to eight weeks.

1. The best way to pot a plant
A pot sherd is placed over the drainage hole and a drainage layer of Hortag provides the right amount of moisture inside the pot.

2. How to remove a plant from its pot

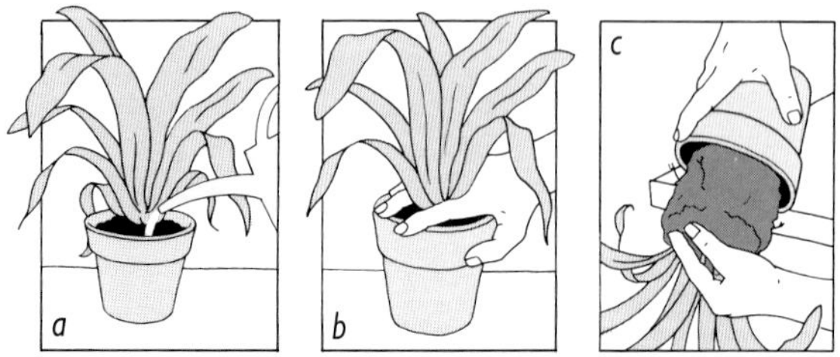

a) Water the plant well two hours before repotting. This will help to loosen the roots from the pot.
b) Lay the palm of your hand on the surface of the soil and hold the plant between two fingers.
c) Turn your hand and the plant upside down and tap the pot against the edge of the table so that the rootstock is loosened inside the pot

How to repot small plants

- Water the plant two hours before repotting so that the rootstock is well moistened (see illustration 2a).
- Lay the palm of your hand on the surface of the soil in such a way that the plant protrudes between two of your fingers (see illustration 2b).
- Holding the plant and pot, turn your hand upside down and carefully tap the edge of the pot against a table top to loosen the rootstock (see illustration 2c).
- Never use force to remove the pot as too many roots could tear. If the rootstock is really stuck inside the pot, it is preferable to break a clay pot carefully with a hammer (see illustration 4a). Plastic pots will require cutting open with robust household scissors.

Repotting large plants

- Water the plant well a few hours before repotting (see illustration 3a).
- Loosen the roots from the walls of the pot with a long knife (see illustration 3b).
- Lay the pot on its side and carefully pull the plant out of the pot. If the roots are still stuck at the bottom of the pot, tap the pot with a piece of wood while turning the pot at the same time. Hold the plant with the other hand (see illustration 3c).

The right way to repot

***Prepare the container*:** Only use thoroughly clean pots for replanting. The new pot should be 3–4 cm (1¼–1¾ in) larger than the old one. Clay pots should be completely submerged in water for one or two hours so that they can soak up water and will not draw moisture from the potting compost later on. Lime deposits can be scrubbed off old pots, using vinegar diluted in water. Alternative: Soaking the pots for three days in peat water will also dissolve the salts.

***Trimming the rootstock*:** The very fine roots are responsible for supplying the plant with water and nutrients, so they should be cut back only if it is absolutely necessary: for example, if:

- the rootstock has developed a densely matted mass of roots. Using scissors, cut off the matted parts around the outside of the rootstock;
- the roots look blackish or glassy and smell bad; usually this means they have decayed. All of these roots need removing but do not cut off any light, beige-coloured, healthy roots.

My tip: If trimming the roots involves cutting the thicker ones, you should dust the latter with charcoal powder so that no germs can invade the tissue.

Remove old soil: Algae, moss and old compost should be crumbled off. With a small stick, carefully remove old soil from the sides and bottom without damaging the fine roots.

Planting: Cover the drainage hole in the pot with a piece of broken pot; insert a 3–5 cm (1¼–2 in) thick drainage layer of Hortag, clay granules or gravel in the bottom of larger pots. Add new compost so that the plant will be sitting at the same height in the new pot as it did before in the old one (see illustration 4b).

Fill the pot and press the compost down lightly, leaving a space of about 2 cm (¾ in) for watering (see illustration 4c).

Aftercare: Place the plant in a bright position with warmth from below – but never in full sunlight. Stand the pot in a dish or pot holder and water the plant well. After about half an hour, pour away any surplus water. Do not fertilize for about six to eight weeks, at the earliest.

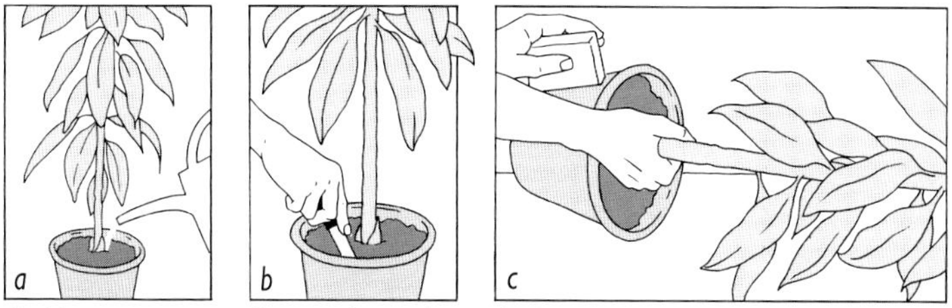

3. How to remove large plants from their pots
a) Water the plant well a few hours before repotting.
b) Loosen the roots from the sides of the pot using a strong knife.
c) Use a chunk of wood to tap the side of the pot and loosen the remaining roots.

Repotting in the same sized pot

If your houseplant has already attained a considerable height and circumference and you cannot give it a larger pot, you should still repot it. There are two alternative methods.

Renew the topmost layer of compost: Using a small stick or spoon, remove the top layer of compost from the pot without damaging the roots. Then refill the pot with new compost.

Cut the rootstock back: Remove the plant from the pot and trim the rootstock slightly all round so that it is smaller. Now you can easily repot the plant with fresh compost in the same, cleaned pot.

NB: Not all plants respond well to this method. If you do not wish to run the risk of losing your plant, I recommend propagating new plants from cuttings or by air layering.

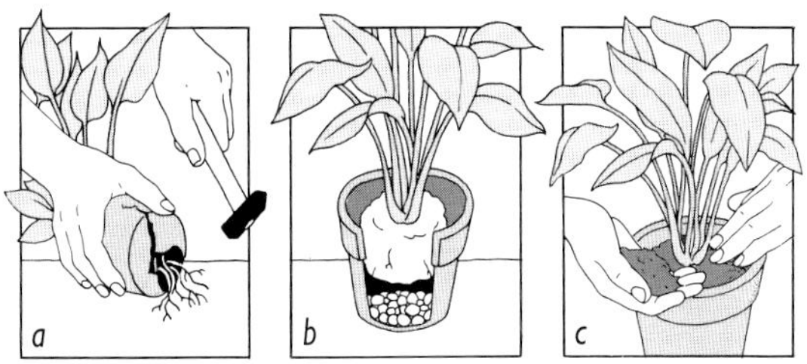

4. Repotting the easy way

a) If the roots are stuck, the last resort is to break a clay pot with a hammer.
b) Insert a drainage layer on top of the pot sherd and set the plant in the pot at the same height as before.
c) Pour in soil and press it down lightly. Leave a 2 cm (¾ in) space for watering.

Peat

When choosing potting compost, you can make a contribution towards protecting the environment. Before you buy, read the packaging to find out the contents of the mixture. This information should be clearly visible, although many potting composts are still offered for sale without any indication of their contents. Choose potting composts:

- that clearly list the contents and components of the compost;
- that are, if possible, free of peat or contain little peat. More and more manufacturers are beginning to offer composts containing less peat. The peat is then replaced with other substances, for example, bark humus, hydromulch and, increasingly, wood fibre whose properties are very similar to those of peat. These composts contain fast-working starter fertilizer. The work of long-term fertilizers is taken over by the organic nutrients contained in the compost or by the addition of controlled-release fertilizers.

There is a wide selection of products for sale in the gardening trade, many of which are suitable for houseplants. Look for commercial potting compost, sold under various brand names, that contains no peat or potting composts that contain very little peat (no more than 40%).

Plant containers

Containers in many shapes and sizes, and made of many different kinds of material, are available for houseplants.

Standard pots all have a drainage hole (or several) to get rid of surplus water. Their size is measured across the diameter at the top. This will also correspond to the height of the pot.

Flat pots (azalea pots) are wider than they are high and are designed for plants whose roots spread sideways.

Narrow, tall pots (palm pots) are ideal for plants whose roots tend to grow downwards.

Bowls and plant basins provide an opportunity of combining several different kinds of plants in a group. The following points should be noted.

- The larger the container, the more important it is to have a drainage layer that is at least 5 cm (2 in) thick so that the roots are not left standing in water after generous watering.
- Only combine species of plants that have the same requirements with respect to water, compost, nutrients, light and temperature. If you do this skilfully, you will soon notice an interesting side effect: the plants tend to do better in groups than singly.

Hanging containers and baskets provide space for several plants if there is no more space on surfaces in the room. These containers are closed at the bottom so that no water can drip out.

NB: Provide the hanging plant with a thick layer of drainage material or place the plant in a special pot so that the hanging container functions as a pot holder. In this case, cover the bottom of the hanging container with a 5 cm (2 in) layer of Hortag, as it is difficult to see into a hanging container to check for surplus water.

Lattice baskets provide an environment close to their natural state for epiphytes such as ferns or bromeliads.

NB: Watering requires some care and thought as the water tends to run right through. The best method is to submerge this kind of plant in water (see p. 30).

Closed terrariums, glass cases or bottle gardens provide the plant communities inside them with an ideal climate for growth and leave them unaffected by the arid air in a room. The water absorbed is then released by the plants through evaporation, condenses on the glass walls and runs back down to the bottom. These plants will hardly require watering. Plant homes of this type are ideal for offices. They are neat, attractive and make few demands with respect to care (see illustration, p. 34).

My tip: Clay pots require more care than plastic pots.

- New clay pots should be cleaned thoroughly before planting to remove any lime deposits, algae or germs. Lime can be removed quite easily with vinegar in water. Rinse well and soak in clean water afterwards.

Ferns in an aquarium – an attractive idea, which also provides the plants with the necessary humidity.

1. Changing over from soil to hydroculture

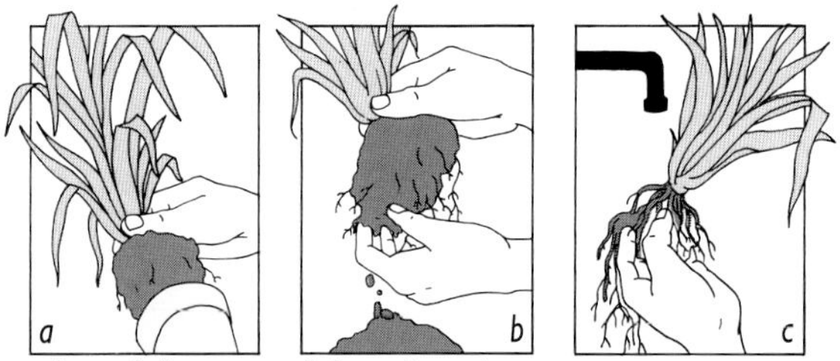

a) Water the plant and carefully remove it from its pot.
b) Gently remove the soil from the roots by hand.
c) Rinse the roots with lukewarm water until all soil has been removed.

Using clay granules

Clay granules are manufactured by different processes so that they may be used in pure hydroculture as well as for combined soil and granule culture.

Hortag (clay granules) can be obtained in the gardening trade in various different sizes. These are the most common granules used in hydroculture, in which plants are grown with their bare roots suspended in Hortag and nutrient solution.

Alternative planting granules make possible a combined cultivation using soil and granules. This involves removing the plant from its pot and simply placing the rootstock still in its soil in the new clay granules.

The advantages of clay granules

- The plant is rarely attacked by pests or disease-inducing organisms that linger in soil because there is no suitable milieu for them.
- They are particularly plant-friendly as their pH value is between 6 and 6.5.
- They are air-permeable, do not become dense and hard and cannot rot.
- They provide the plant with optimal amounts of oxygen, water and nutrients.
- Mistakes in watering are almost impossible as a water level indicator in hydroculture, and moisture meters in the case of other plant granules, will indicate when they need more water.
- Plants cultivated in this fashion are ideal for offices. The water supply will usually last for about one to two weeks, so they will not need watering very often. Fertilizing is a similar matter: special long-lasting fertilizers ensure that you only need to fertilize every four to six months in hydroculture, and every two months in the case of other plant granules.

Before changing to hydroculture

Changing from soil cultivation to hydroculture is possible – but not with all plants and there is always a risk involved. Before making the attempt, you should realize that such a change brings an initial shock for the plant as it is suddenly forced to adapt its entire root activity and nutritional needs to hydroculture.

- Sickly or weak plants will rarely survive the ordeal.
- Older plants also rarely cope with the change.
- Not every plant is suited to hydroculture (see tables, pp. 10–11 and 14–15). Leafy plants cope better than flowering plants.
- Plants with many fine roots find it harder to adapt.
- The best chances of success can be expected in the case of young plants with robust, thick roots, such as the flamingo flower (*Anthurium*), *Chlorophytum*, *Hoya* and *Schefflera*.

2. Setting the plant in an alternative medium
Rinse the medium well and allow it to soak up water. Set the plant roots, with their soil, in the new medium, no deeper than previously. Insert a moisture meter in the rootstock.

Changing over to hydroculture

Essential tools

- a container;
- water level meter;
- a pot holder;
- Hortag, which should be thoroughly rinsed before use and allowed to soak up water.

Water the plant and carefully remove it from its pot (see illustration 1a). Do not damage the roots; if necessary, break the pot or cut it open.
Carefully remove loose soil (see illustration 1b). You may gently pull the rootstock apart to remove as much soil as possible.
Rinse off any remaining soil (see illustration 1c) with lukewarm, soft, running water. If possible, allow the roots to soak overnight. The soil must be completely removed from the roots or they will begin to decay in hydroculture.
Only cut off bent, diseased or decayed parts of roots.
Insert Hortag into the culture vessel.
NB: The granules should be well rinsed and soaked before use. The container can be any size. Insert a 3–5 cm (1¼–2 in) layer of Hortag in the bottom.
Hold the plant in the container so that it sits no deeper than before. Spread out the roots and allow the Hortag to slide in gently.
Shake the container gently so that the Hortag is dispersed properly. On no account press the Hortag down.
Insert the water level indicator and stand the plant in a pot holder.
Pour in clear, hand-warm water, but not so much that the roots are left standing in water.

NB: Place a transparent plastic hood over the plant and seal it well. This ensures that high humidity is maintained. If the inside of the bag develops condensation, you should air it daily for about fifteen minutes. The position chosen should be bright (but not sunny) and the plant should be kept warm from below. A warming mat placed under the plant is excellent. As soon as the plant starts to produce new shoots, you can remove the hood and begin to add low doses of special nutrient solution.

3. Repotting in hydroculture
a) Lift the plant from the container and remove old Hortag granules.
b) Fill a new container to a depth of 3–5 cm (1¼–2 in) with new Hortag.
c) Set the plant in the container and fill the container with Hortag all the way round.
d) Insert the water level indicator and pour in water mixed with a suitable nutrient solution *(see p. 42)*

Repotting in hydroculture

Houseplants grown in hydroculture quickly develop a dense root system. If you place them in large containers, you will not need to repot them every year. It is time to repot when the roots have filled the container.

- Remove the plant from its container and gently remove the Hortag (see illustration 3a).
- Clean the new container thoroughly, rinse it and allow it to soak.
- Insert a 3–5 cm (1¼–2 in) layer of Hortag and set the plant at the same depth as before (illustration 3b).
- Carefully distribute the granules around the plant and shake the container a little so that they are distributed more evenly (see illustration 3c).
- Insert the water level indicator and pour in the nutrient solution (see illustration 3d).

Repotting in alternative clay granules

With this type of culture (see illustration 2), the plant, its rootstock and soil are simply replanted in the new clay medium. According to the manufacturers, this is possible with all plants. The best time for repotting is early spring to autumn.
Fill a third of a closed container with well-rinsed granules. Place the plant, together with its soil and rootstock, in the container and fill it up with more granules. Insert the moisture meter into the root area and pour in water containing the special liquid fertilizer.

Flowering plants in a south-facing summer window

Plants that will thrive in a sunny window during the summer are the sun-worshippers, such as desert cacti and succulents – plants that are able to store water in their stems or fleshy leaves and can cope with lots of sunlight.

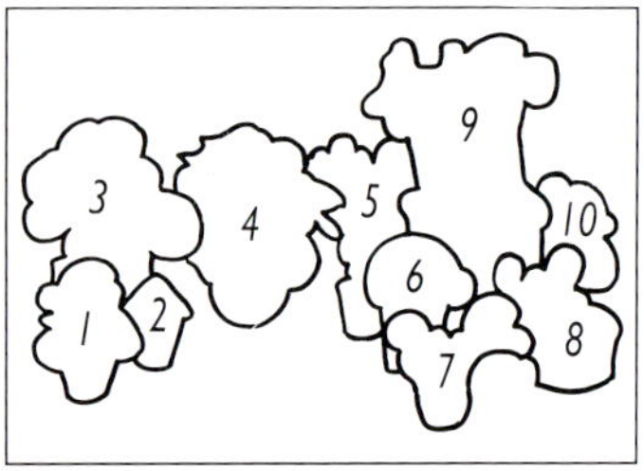

Plants in a south-facing window *(from left to right):*
1. *Kalanchoë blossfeldiana*
2. *Echeveria*
3. *Bougainvillea glabra*
4. *blue passion flower (Passiflora caerulea)*
5. *Mandevilla hybrid*
6. *Sonerila margaritacea*
7. *Kalanchoë blossfeldiana*
8. *Desert cactus (Opuntia microdasys) (left), Echinocactus grusonii (front right), Cereus jamacaru (back)*
9. *lemon tree (Citrus limon)*
10. *Hibiscus rosa-sinensis*

First aid

Mistakes in care will often result in problems or disease. However, if you apply first aid quickly, you can generally restore your plants to health.

Sun burn.

Brown spots on the leaves

Irregular spots on slightly wavy leaves indicate burns. Immediately remove the plant from direct sunlight.

My tip: A bad sunburn can also cause large, silvery, clearly defined spots on the leaves.

Brown leaf tips and edges

These are unmistakable signs of arid air. Increase the humidity immediately. Several courses of action are possible (see pp. 34–35).

Falling leaves

This is caused by too little light or not enough nutrients. The plant may also be suffering from damage to the roots (for example, waterlogging) so that it is no longer able to sustain its parts above ground. The plant must be removed from its pot. Cut off any decayed roots and plant it in fresh potting compost. Depending on the extent of the damage, the plant may have a chance of surviving.

Falling leaves.

Iron deficiency.

Yellow leaves with green veins

This plant is suffering from lack of iron. This can be most quickly remedied by using a preparation containing iron, which is sprayed on to the leaves. Water the plant with soft water only. Iron deficiency usually occurs if the water contains too much lime. This forms compounds with the iron so that the plant no longer has access to it.

My tip: Similar symptoms appear with a lack of magnesium. In that case, the areas around the veins remain green.

Completely dry.

Limp leaves and shoots

The plant is suffering from lack of water and it is high time to water it. Usually, the rootstock is so dried out that it can no longer absorb water. The only thing that will save the plant now is a long soak (see p. 30).

Rolled-up leaves

This plant is trying to cut down on water loss through evaporation by curling up its leaves. The reasons may be manifold. For example, a position in too much sunlight, arid air or too little water. Put things right immediately.

First aid

A recipe for success
Even sickly houseplants will became strong and healthy again if they are allowed to spend time outside in the summer. Place them on your balcony or patio – but only after carefu acclimatization in the shade.

Campanula isophylla can tolerate water that contains lime and should be placed in a bright position outside during the summer.

Index

Figures in bold indicate illustrations.

Index

Index

Index

Acknowledgements
The author and publishers wish to thank Karin Greiner of the Institut für Botanisch-ökologische Beratung, Munich, for her invaluable advice.

Author's note
This book deals with the care of houseplants. Some of the plants described here are partially or completely toxic. Any toxic plants, which might cause serious harm to the health of adults or children, have been marked with a warning symbol in the tables on pp. 10–11 and 14–15. Please make absolutely sure that children and pets are not able to eat the plants designated in this way.
When using plant protection agents, always follow the instructions on the packaging meticulously and also the recommendations on p. 23. Store all plant protection agents and fertilizers (including organic ones such as horn chips, bonemeal, algae, lime, guano and crushed volcanic rock) in a place that is inaccessible to children and pets, as their consumption may be harmful to health. None of these substances should be allowed to come into contact with your eyes. If open wounds are sustained during contact with soil, you should visit a doctor for professional advice and to discuss the possibility of having a tetanus vaccination.

Cover photographs
Front cover: main picture, *Euphorbia pulcherrima*; top right, *Begonia hiemalis*; middle right, *Saintpaulia ionantha*; bottom right, *Schlumberga*.
Inside front cover: *lemon balm, parsley, chives, thyme and mint.*
Inside back cover: *tools and equipment for looking after houseplants.*
Back cover: *Spathiphyllum wallisii.*

Photographic acknowledgements
Becherer: p. 41; Lynne Brotchie, Garden Picture Library: front cover centre, bottom right; Eisenbeiss: p. 8 top left, 12 right, 13 top left, 13 top centre; Juliet Green, Garden Picture Library: back cover; Henseler: p. 20 top left, 20 top right, 21 top right, 21 bottom, 58 top left, 58 top right, 58 bottom; Merehurst Ltd: inside front cover; Photoplant: p. 17; Schfer: p. 21 top centre left, 21 top centre right; Schneiders: p. 4–5, 9 right, 12 left, 24–25, 29, 32, 36–37, 44–45, 48, 56–57, 59, inside back cover; Silvestris/Riedmiller: p. 13 top right; Stork: p. 1 top centre left, 1 top centre right, 1 top right, 1 bottom, 20 bottom, 53, 58 top centre; Friedrich Strauss, Garden Picture Library: front cover, top right, middle right; Strauss: p. 1 top left, 8 top centre, 8 top right, 8 bottom, 9 left, 13 bottom; Zunke: p. 21 top left.

This edition published 1994 by
Merehurst Limited
Ferry House, 51–57 Lacy Road,
Putney, London SW15 1PR

Reprinted 1997, 2000

ISBN 1 85391 920 9

A catalogue record for this book is available from the British Library.

Translated by Astrid Mick
Edited by Lesley Young
Design and typesetting by
Cooper Wilson Design
Printed in Hong Kong by Wing King Tong